PREACHING
WHILE THE CHURCH
IS UNDER
*R*ECONSTRUCTION

PREACHING
WHILE THE CHURCH IS UNDER
$\mathcal{R}$ECONSTRUCTION

The Visionary Role of Preachers in
a Fragmented World

Thomas H. Troeger

ABINGDON PRESS
NASHVILLE

PREACHING WHILE THE CHURCH IS UNDER RECONSTRUCTION

Library of Congress Cataloging-in-Publication Data

Troeger, Thomas H., 1945-
     Preaching while the church is under reconstruction : the visionary role of preachers in a fragmented world / Thomas H. Troeger.
     p. cm.
     ISBN 0-687-08549-7 (pbk. : alk. paper)
     1. Preaching. 2. Church renewal. I. Title.
     BV4211.2.T7654   1999
     251—dc21   98-48163
                                                                        CIP

Copyright page continues on page 176

99 00 01 02 03 04 05 06 07 08— 10 9 8 7 6 5 4 3 2 1

For my mother,
who taught me to know God
through her twin passions for the Bible and poetry

for my father,
who taught me to know God
through his twin passions for science and music

with thanksgiving for the grace they shared;
honoring each other's different ways to God
and allowing them to flow with equal power
into my heart

Contents

Acknowledgments

I am grateful to many preachers, students, and colleagues who have listened to various portions of this book while it was in process and to their schools, organizations, and churches that invited me to lecture and lead seminars and conferences. Their responses were crucial to the development of the manuscript. I thank the Academy of Homiletics, especially Mary Ann Wiesemann-Mills, O.P., and Professor Joseph Webb; the Florida Winter Pastors' School of Stetson University; Moravian Theological Seminary and its Alumni/ae Association; Lee Everding and her Eclectics public forum; Wake Forest University Divinity School; Societas Homiletica, with special thanks to Professors Tsuneaki Kato and Robert Fukada; the Association of Disciples Musicians; Chautauqua Institute; Old Stone Church of Cleveland; Dubuque University; the University of Utrecht, with special thanks to Professor Gerrit Immink and Pastor Jan Chr. Vaessen; First Presbyterian Church of Albuquerque; the Consortium of Endowed Episcopal Parishes; the Mumford Memorial Lectureship at Queen's Theological College in Kingston, Ontario; my stimulating and diverse classes at Iliff, with special thanks to my research assistant, Charla Gwartney, and to my colleagues there who either read the manuscript or helped to talk through the issues, especially Delwin Brown, Edward Everding, Dennis McDonald, and Dana Wilbanks; my pastors of many years who inspire me by their leadership of the church under reconstruction, Sarah Butler, Charles Kiblinger, Elizabeth Randall; and above all my wife Merle Marie, whose unfailing grace to me is a daily witness to the living Christ.

Remembering the lively interest of all these people gives me hope for the future. Their faces and voices and their visions of a reconstructed church were vividly present to me as I wrote. They are a living witness of what it means to bring all that we are—including our minds—to the praise and service of God. I take courage from their willingness to seek new theological understandings as an act of faithfulness to the living Spirit, the sovereign wind that blows in ways we can never control and that continually surprise us.

T. H. T.
Denver,
Colorado
Lent 1998

Chapter 1

The Church Under Reconstruction

A PARABLE

Some said
there had been too much rain
and the roof
long cracked after years of stress
gave way from water seeping in.

Others said
what fell from the heavens
had nothing to do with it,
that the earth had shifted
and the church walls
had pushed out toward the city market
so that the massive mosaic of the Almighty Father
had fallen in and left a hole,
a silhouette of the icon

that used to command the whole church
from high above the nave.

Services now
were held under the God-shaped hole:
prayers said
hymns sung
infants baptized
sermons preached
offerings made
communion celebrated
couples wed
the dead remembered.

Meanwhile reconstruction began,
but it turned out harder than planned.

Some folks had taken home
bits of the original mosaic
as a piece of devotion or historical curiosity,
and when it was discovered
there was not enough left to restore
the original ancient grandeur
debates erupted if they should even try
to recreate what was lost.

Some said
they should begin and finish the project
as quickly as possible
because people were not coming as they used to
since the icon had collapsed.

Others pointed out
new people were entering the church
curious about the place
in a way they never were before.
And these newcomers joined
with those who had always been scared

by the icon's fierce eyes
to suggest they replace the old image
with a new one.

The differences about what to do
broke into conflict
so that for now the construction
was nearly halted,
though some workers
tried to assemble the roof in bits and pieces.

But without an overall plan
nothing would stay put.
Even the stars that surrounded the hole
began to fall from the ceiling
so that another party arose
suggesting they take down the entire
edifice and start all over anew—

except that the most devout
could not bear to lose this or that altar
where they had prayed so long
and the stones were worn smooth
by the knees of many generations.

So for the time being
all that was done
was to rope off the area beneath
the God-shaped hole
to make sure no one was hit by a piece of mosaic
that would fall from time to time
from a cracked angel or star
and to pray
that people would keep coming
while the church continued to be,
as the sign alerting those who entered said:

Under Reconstruction.[1]

13

THE LOSS OF COMMANDING CERTITUDE

I have shared this parable with many different audiences: local pastors, lay leaders, church musicians, professors of homiletics, and seminary students. It awakens a range of responses from anger to appreciation, from fear to prayer.

I recall a preacher who identified himself as "a pastor of a tall-steeple church." His congregation of several thousand had drifted in the last few decades "toward an increasing conservatism bordering on fundamentalism."

"Your story frightens me," he said, "because although my church does not yet worship under 'the God-shaped hole,' the first cracks are appearing. I think the roof is going to fall on me and a lot of others who have been denying the change that is happening." He explained that several women whose workplaces mandated inclusive language in their official documents had asked him to make his sermons more inclusive. Other church members were attracted to the popularization of scholarship about Jesus and the perspectives opened by new critical approaches to the Bible. Still others were noticing that their much heralded church growth made them "look like a country club" with constricted membership qualifications.

Although frightened by the parable of the hole in the church roof, the pastor also found hope in it. "The story is not about the death of God," he said. He took it to be a parable about the collapse of a particular image of God and the constellations of symbol and interpretation that radiate from the image. The parable for him was about the crumbling of a certain dome of meaning and about the necessity of opening himself anew to the living Spirit of God.

The pastor was beginning to acknowledge to

14

himself, if not to his congregation, that preaching nowadays takes place in an edifice of thought and belief which is marked by an unmistakable incompleteness. There are still standing walls and definable space, but there has been a loss of commanding certitude so that preachers are challenged to work toward a new imagining. How do we preach in a church under reconstruction, a church in which many Christians are rebuilding their understanding of belief, worship, and ministry?

INSTITUTIONAL REALISM

There are many pastors and church consultants who answer that question by saying: We first need to address the institutional realities of the church, its diminished status in North American society, and the shrinking of its material resources. We need to be institutional realists, coming to terms with new paradigms of the church, the rise of the megachurches, and the "church growth movement." This response takes seriously that

the church has been in a process of relocation for some time now and we are just coming to admit it. The church is socially dwarfed by other institutions; it is no longer deferred to. Its marginality cuts into the desire of those who want to be a part of majority culture. To be honest, we have to admit that on any given Sunday most members of mainline churches are just a few centimetres away from not attending. The tradition of regular, weekly attendance is no longer automatic.[2]

Institutional viability is an essential matter. I am indebted to the Alban Institute and the Center for Parish Development for their sophisticated analyses of the group life of congregations and the conditions that foster a healthy, faithful church. One of the things that is so attractive to me about their literature and conferences is how they affirm the necessity of thinking imaginatively about the church and its future. Loren Mead puts the matter boldly:

> The forms and structures, the roles and relationships of the churches we have inherited were formed by paradigms that no longer work for us. We live in the memory of great ways of understanding how to be church and to be in mission. Those memories surround us like ruins of an ancient civilization. Our educational institutions and our structures of leadership and service are likewise conflicted and at war with themselves.
>
> How do we build religious institutions within which we can live out our calling to serve the world? How do we form ourselves for mission to the emerging age?[3]

Mead believes that *"our task is no less than the reinvention of the church. It may take several generations. We will not see the end of it, but we must begin now."*[4]

I like the metaphor "reinvention" because it suggests the need for novelty, for creating the church anew. However, I am also taken with the metaphor of "reconstruction" because it honors the church walls that are still standing, broken as they are, and because it reminds us of the heavy labor involved. Although I will use "reconstruction" throughout this book, the truth of our situation is probably in a blend of the metaphors. We need the reinvention/ reconstruction of the church. In both cases the prefix "re" is significant because it reminds us that we are not starting from scratch: we have a tradition that supplies many, though not all, of the materials required for reinventing and reconstructing the church.

I will focus on one essential part of this major undertaking: the visionary role of preachers in a fragmented world. By "fragmented world" I mean the brokenness of relationships, institutions, and theological understandings that pastors report to me everywhere I lead conferences in North America.

By "visionary role," I mean the public function of preachers to give witness to God with an imaginative power that vitalizes the faith and ministry of the congregation.

Wladimir Weidle has written that "when the real world threatens to collapse" we may question the wisdom of spending our energies on the work of the imagination, but in fact the matter "is not as simple as one might at first be inclined to think" because whatever "impedes" our imaginations "may connect with deeper causes, causes more worthy of attention than all the other woes that befall us."[5] The truth of Weidle's insight came home to me when I presented material from this book to a Protestant congregation during a weekend of leadership training. All of them were strong churchgoers, ranging in age from twenty to eighty. They were not frightened by the parable of the God-shaped hole. As one of them explained: "It gives me a way to name what I have felt for some time now in church."

When I identified the need for revitalizing the spiritual imagination of the church, they responded with strong affirmation. They had no trouble seeing that a major cause of our fragmentation is the atrophy of the church's ability to present a compelling sense of the reality of God. They came alive at the opportunity to discuss the theology and spiritual life of the church.

PRELUDE TO PREACHING:
WAITING AND WORSHIPING

I recounted to that Protestant congregation a Roman Catholic sister's earlier response to the question: How do we preach while the church is under reconstruction, a church in which many Christians

17

are rebuilding their understanding of belief, worship, and ministry?

"We do nothing immediately. We sit underneath the hole and wait."

Mary Ann Wiesemann-Mills, O.P., welcomed "the unbounded possibilities" that were opened by the God-shaped hole. She believed it was essential that we not rush too quickly through the "impasse" of conflicting images, but that we live with them "as a way of moving more deeply into the mystery of God who holds us in her womb."[6] When I related the sister's response to the Protestant congregation, they nodded their heads in agreement. They had a sense that the "solution" to our fragmentation lies in something more than busyness. Techniques of growth and vitalization must be rooted in prayer, in a willingness to wait upon the Spirit.

Preaching while the church is under reconstruction does not begin with homiletical method but with prayer, with a willingness to live with the God-shaped hole rather than rushing to fill it up with the inadequate projections of our nervous hearts. Visionary preachers realize that "their leadership must be unabashedly religious and spiritual."[7] What Jung Young Lee writes about Korean preaching is true for all who preach while the church is under reconstruction: "Prayers and preaching are inseparable. Preaching without a prayerful and meditative attitude may become a beautiful, sweet talk, but it cannot be authentic and prophetic preaching. The prayer life of the minister and the congregation is, therefore, the foundation of effective preaching."[8]

We open ourselves to visions and voices from the cloud of witnesses (Hebrews 11:1–12:1) borne by the wind of the Spirit that will guide us "into all the truth" (John 16:13). This requires theological courage and a conviction that even if the canon is closed the revelatory work of the Spirit continues: "The word is not limited to what is known of God through creation, or history, or scripture. But God present in the Holy Spirit discloses the new word, the distinctive word, the word addressed to this particular situation."[9] While we wait upon the Spirit, we continue to worship in the church under reconstruction, using the richness of scripture and tradition that we have inherited.

Services now
are held under the God-shaped hole:
prayers said
hymns sung
infants baptized
sermons preached
offerings made
communion celebrated
couples wed
the dead remembered.

We view our worship as "primary theology," believing that "the gathered church at prayer is doing theology, from which more abstract forms of critical reflection and 'secondary theology' emerge."[10] The history of our primary theology reveals that the church has nearly always been under reconstruction. Many of those things which we now most cherish in our services grew out of theological turmoil every bit as intense and bitter as our own time. They were created by people who in a fragmented world had a gift for presenting the word of God with visionary power. Take, for example, the hymns of the church, "the poor person's poetry and the ordinary person's theology."[11] We often fight against any changes to them as though the hymn texts and their musical settings were established from the beginning of the world. But if we study the circumstances of their creation, we will usually

> find ourselves looking at the church in times of crisis and of tension. Not that the church has spent much of its time in any other condition—but hymns, we shall find, have flourished most vigorously on the far edges of the church: at what some might call its growing points and others its vulnerable or even heretical points. The pattern forms itself at once: periods when somebody somewhere is tearing up the turf and asking questions and organizing rebellions and reconstructing disciplines produce hymns . . .[12]

- Because hymns were most often produced while the church was under reconstruction
- because hymns frequently pointed to new images and understandings of the Christian faith
- because hymns were often written by preachers, theologians, and common folk working to find the meaning of faith for their age
- because hymns frequently expressed the church's emerging new identity and mission
- because hymns use poetic compression, saying a lot in a few memorable stanzas
- and because hymns often capture the homiletical themes of their age yet are more available to most of us than historic collections of sermons

they can help us understand the visionary role of preachers in a fragmented world. And this is by no means true only of Protestantism. For "although Martin Luther gave hymnody a 'new start,' there is a sense in which Latin hymnody [which begins with Ambrose, bishop of Milan, 340–397] is the source of all the rest."[13] Hymns are like the sample borings of geologists: they allow us to dig down through the layers of church history to get a representative sample of the stresses and strains, the sediments and crystallizations that characterized the topography of faith in the past. The capacity to illuminate visionary preaching in a church under reconstruction extends not only to hymns but also to spirituals, poems, prayers, legends, sermons, visual and dramatic presentations of the gospel. There are witnesses in the cloud who still speak to us through this diversity of media. Their varied means of expression remind us that part of our visionary role is to amplify our repertoire of methods for communicating the gospel of Christ.

THE HISTORY OF FAITH: THE HISTORY OF GOD-SHAPED HOLES

When I wait prayerfully beneath the God-shaped hole, I hear the wind of the Spirit and thunder from the cloud reminding me that our age is not the first time the dome of meaning has collapsed. Wind and cloud bring back the memory of faithful people who long before us struggled to find meaning in a fragmented world. The history of faith is the history of God-shaped holes. It is the story of believers thinking they understood God only to discover the inadequacy of their theological formulation. Every time their image of God crumbled, the Wind blew, the Spirit stirred prophet, poet, and preacher to a more expansive understanding of God. That new image then dominated the dome of meaning until it too crumbled and the Wind blew yet again.

The congregated light of the past shines from the cloud of witnesses. Their wisdom is now shaped not only by their time on earth but also by the transfiguration of perspective that comes through viewing mortal life from the cloud. Opening ourselves to their viewpoint involves an imaginative

21

appropriation of the past: we study what our ancestors did and thought, then play creatively with the
inheritance they left behind.

Sometimes it seems as though the last thing we
need to do is to return to consider tradition, because "while tradition is an important anchor in any
community, it, along with church laws, has the
potential to stunt innovation."[14] Tradition, however,
is far more than an "anchor." Tradition is also a
"cloud" of witnesses. Look at the difference between those images.

An anchor is buried in the bottom of the sea,
holding us in place. But a cloud forms and reforms
with the play of wind and light. An anchor may
"stunt innovation," but not a "cloud." The cloud of
witnesses reminds us that reality will not stay put.
The cloud reveals that tradition is a dynamic
process, that tradition initiates creativity, that tradition gives our imaginations depth and wisdom by
connecting us to a greater base of human experience than the puny little domain of the present
moment. Knowledge of the past feeds our imaginations and stimulates our visionary energies for
preaching in a fragmented age. When I play with the
past, I hear thunder from the cloud:

"'Tis all in pieces, all coherence gone."

It is John Donne (1572–1631), one of the finest
Christian poet/preachers in the English language.
That I should hear an English poet/preacher reveals
something of my particular past, the way I was
raised by my mother reading the King James Version
of the Bible and reciting English poetry to me
throughout my childhood, an upbringing amplified
by my education. Although I treasure the traditions
in which I was raised and although much of my
imaginative energy flows from them, I do not

assume that the witnesses from the cloud who speak to me are the same who speak to you. The more I am exposed to other cultures and backgrounds the more I come to see the truth of Ada Maria Isasi-Diaz's observation: "I learned to distrust those who claim objectivity, which in my view is merely the subjectivity of those who have the power to impose it on others."[15] My goal is not to impose my subjectivity upon you, but to model a creative way of gathering from our ancestors visionary power to preach while the church is under reconstruction. My hope is that the witnesses who inspire me will invoke the witnesses who inspire you. For the cloud is far vaster than any one individual, race, nation, or religious tradition.

Stop.
Imagine the cloud.
Who emerges from the cloud for you?
What wisdom do they have that you need?
Let them join in the conversation.
Hear them intermingling, correcting and affirming my witnesses from the cloud.

" 'Tis all in pieces, all coherence gone."

Donne's words keep sounding from the cloud in my heart, keep reverberating beneath the God-shaped hole. While Donne preached and wrote, the scientific revolution was gaining momentum. New cosmologies and global exploration were throwing ancient authorities into question, fracturing established meanings and values:

And freely men confess that this world's spent,
When in the planets, and the firmament
They seek so many new; then see that this
Is crumbled out again to his atomies.
'Tis all in pieces, all coherence gone;
All just supply, and all relation:
Prince, subject, Father, Son are things forgot.[16]

'Tis all in pieces, pieces, pieces, all coherence gone, gone, gone. The words echo off the walls of the church with the God-shaped hole and awaken more thunder and voices from the cloud. No one age has a monopoly on God-shaped holes. Other witnesses rush from the cloud to remind us how theirs was an era of immense theological turmoil. I hear the voice of a psalmist who lived through devastating circumstances:

> In the LORD I take refuge; how can you say to me,
>> "Flee like a bird to the mountains;
> for look, the wicked bend the bow,
>> they have fitted their arrow to the string,
>> to shoot in the dark at the upright in heart.
> If the foundations are destroyed,
>> what can the righteous do?"
>
> The LORD is in his holy temple;
>> the LORD's throne is in heaven.
>> His eyes behold, his gaze examines humankind.
> The LORD tests the righteous and the wicked,
>> and his soul hates the lover of violence.
> On the wicked he will rain coals of fire and sulfur;
>> a scorching wind shall be the portion of their cup.
> For the LORD is righteous;
> he loves righteous deeds;
>> the upright shall behold his face. (Psalm 11)

The ancient poet suggests three different ways of responding when "the foundations are destroyed," or as another translation puts it, "When the world falls apart" (Psalm 11:3*a*).[17] All three of the psalmist's responses are possibilities for preachers nowadays. The first is escape. An unidentified voice counsels the psalmist "Flee like a bird to the mountains" (Psalm 11:1). And why not? Things are bad. The city streets are filled with violence. There are nighttime shootings. It is not safe to walk the neighborhood anymore. Flee! How tempting for us preachers to offer the same counsel by providing old-time religion, by refusing to deal with the fact that "the foundations are destroyed," that "the world falls apart," that the dome of meaning has a God-shaped hole. Flee like a bird to the mountains and hide there as comfortably as people hide in their gated communities and second homes. "Give me that old-time religion."

Flight was the temptation of the preacher whose church had drifted "toward an increasing conservatism bordering on fundamentalism." And yet he had enough awareness to realize that the strategy was beginning to break down, because, although his church "does not yet worship under 'the God-shaped hole,' the first cracks are appearing."

The psalmist refuses to flee because God is his "refuge," but in the course of affirming his faith, he reveals another equally inadequate response. While decrying the violence in the streets, the psalmist pictures God as a God of violence, a firebombing deity who "on the wicked . . . will rain coals of fire and sulfur" (Psalm 11:6).

The temptation for exegetes is to explain away the violent language about God as hyperbole, idiomatic biblical speech that serves to convey God's moral fervor. But no amount of exegetical exactitude can remove the fact that fanatical believers appeal to such language for evil ends. They use it to justify their crusades against those whom they would eliminate from the human community. As Mieke Bal has observed: "The Bible, of all books, is the most dangerous one, the one that has been endowed with the power to kill."[18] Whatever the shape of a reconstructed church, we do not want it to be a house of meaning in which the Bible or any other symbol functions as a lethal weapon. In the final verse, the psalmist turns from flight and violence to "righteous deeds" (Psalm 11:7), to acting with integrity even when "the foundations are destroyed."

The psalm portrays the struggle that goes on beneath the God-shaped hole:

From flight
to fight
to right.

If we wait patiently and listen to the cloud and the Wind, then we may be less driven by panic, less apt to close the opening prematurely and to project our fears upon those who are different from us. Then the cloud and Wind may empower us to live faithfully, to act rightly, to fill our role as visionary preachers.

THE NEATLY ORDERED
INTER-RELATED HIERARCHIES

I hear weeping from the cloud: our ancestors are mourning how they resorted to escape or violence when the domes of meaning that arched over their mortal existence collapsed. They repent and are changed in ways beyond our calculation. The transformation of our ancestors is suggested by biblical passages that reflect "the widespread Hellenistic belief that humans are changed as a result of beholding the divine."[19] What hope is symbolized in that ancient belief: that our ancestors would mourn their errors if they were privileged to gain a perspective from which they could see them, and they would be transformed. We can graciously extend to our ancestors the same honor that we hope future generations will extend to us when they plainly see those faults which elude our current perception. The tears of the cloud are a gift to us preachers. They beckon us away from doing harm with our words, from claiming for God what is nothing more than the projection of our own needs and fears. We do not want to appear as believers who keep their "theologies at their ready like rifles."[20] Theologically fed violence is the abnegation of the gospel of grace.

Among our weeping ancestors are the doctors of the church who on February 19, 1616, declared absurd and foolish the Copernican view, supported by Galileo, that the earth circles the sun. It contradicted the Bible and the teachings of the church. But now from the cloud, the mistaken doctors of theology understand what a later scholar would write about the fears that drove their pronouncement:

> By challenging the traditional view of the universe, Galileo upset *the psychological security that derived from the neatly ordered inter-related hierarchies* of astronomy, philosophy and theology. His opponents were afraid that if the geocentric concept fell, the whole construct of cosmology, the truth of the Scriptures and the anthropocentrism of creation would have to fall with it.[21]

The words "the psychological security that derived from the neatly ordered inter-related hierarchies" echo over and over against the walls of church with the God-shaped hole. They remind us of all the terrors perpetuated by misguided faith. They sound at the mention of every heretic's name, at the memory of every torture, burning, and lynching blessed by preachers who, claiming to have a word from God, were in truth protecting the security that derived from their "neatly ordered inter-related hierarchies."

OPEN TRUTH TO THE SOUL

Not every believer and preacher has panicked when a God-shaped hole appeared in the dome of meaning. Even though not fully convinced that Galileo was right, Tommaso Campanella (1568–1639), defended as a principle of faith the astronomer's right to continue unimpeded his scientific work. Campanella wrote that one who participates in open inquiry "does not impugn faith, but rather, opens truth to the soul." For "it is an essential part of the glory of the Christian religion that we permit [Galileo's] method of discovering new knowledge and of rectifying the old."[22]

The phrase "opens truth to the soul" sounds beneath the God-shaped hole as loudly as "the neatly ordered inter-related hierarchies." The two phrases and their variations begin to alternate until they become a chorus of antiphonal thunder that reiterates itself age after age. We sense the immense struggle between two contradictory ways that faith has functioned through history:

> Protect the hierarchies.
> Open truth to the soul.
> Protect the hierarchies.
> Open truth to the soul.

The alternating declarations resonate with the struggles we find in scripture. The Bible appears to be a musical score composed by multiple composers who write variations on these two motifs again and again:

> Protect the hierarchies.
> Open truth to the soul.
> Protect the hierarchies.
> Open truth to the soul.

When, for example, Babylon destroyed the temple and led the Israelites into exile in 587 B.C.E., it created a gigantic God-shaped hole because the inviolability of the temple had been an article of faith for many believers. Furthermore, it was believed Yahweh had a special relationship to the land and particularly to the temple in Jerusalem.

28

With the destruction of Yahweh's "dwelling place," Yahweh's power was called into question. Some scrambled to fill the God-shaped hole with a passionate avowal of loyalty to past glories:

> If I forget you, O Jerusalem, let my right hand wither!
> Let my tongue cling to the roof of my mouth,
>   if I do not remember you,
> if I do not set Jerusalem above my highest joy.
>   (Psalm 137:5-6)

Not content to promise undying loyalty to the memory of Jerusalem, the psalmist invokes a curse upon the destroyers: "Happy shall they be who take your little ones and dash them against the rock!" (Psalm 137:9). By promise and curse the psalmist maintains, at least in his memory, the psychological security that derived from the neatly ordered inter-related hierarchies of popular belief.[23] It was left to more visionary preachers, Jeremiah, Ezekiel, and Isaiah (or the prophets whose words bear his name) to open truth to the soul, to respond more creatively to the gigantic God-shaped hole left by the exile. Instead of a deity tied to a geographic location, Isaiah expands the divine domain:

> Have you not known? Have you not heard?
>   Has it not been told you from the beginning?
>   Have you not understood from the foundations of
>   the earth?
> It is he who sits above the circle of the earth,
>   and its inhabitants are like grasshoppers;
> who stretches out the heavens like a curtain,
>   and spreads them like a tent to live in;
> who brings princes to naught,
>   and makes the rulers of the earth as nothing.
>   (Isaiah 40:21-23)

Instead of giving people old-time religion, the prophet dares them to amplify their understanding of God and the world.

The process of theological reconstruction in the presence of God-shaped holes continues in the New Testament. The community of John the evangelist was facing a collapse of theological meaning some three generations after Jesus' ministry:

- Christ had not returned.
- The reign of God had not been fulfilled.
- Things had turned bitter with the established religious community.
- There were people beginning to doubt the resurrection and to withdraw from the worship (John 20:24).
- And there was a need to stop clasping the Jesus they had known in order to accept the Christ who was greater than their familiar beliefs (John 20:17).

The cumulative result was a God-shaped hole in their dome of meaning. The Jesus traditions they had inherited were inadequate to fill it. So John and his church became visionary preachers to themselves and wrote their own gospel. It was a community project, a gospel offering new interpretations of Christ that made sense out of their life together.

Theological reconstruction was for John's church an act of faithfulness to the risen Christ whose "first post resurrection teaching" is " 'Do not hold on to me' (John 20:17): When he speaks these words, Jesus teaches Mary that he cannot and will not be held and controlled. One cannot hold Jesus to preconceived standards and expectations of who he should be, because to do so is to interfere with Jesus' work and thereby limit what Jesus has to offer."[24]

The theological audacity of John and Isaiah suggests that to be biblical does not mean to retreat to the language of the past when the dome of meaning collapses.

- To be biblical is to be as courageous as prophet and evangelist were.
- To be biblical is to realize that "The Bible is not God, nor is it a substitute for God, and to treat it as if it were God or a surrogate of God is to treat it in the very way that it itself condemns over and over again."[25]
- To be biblical is to be honest about the Bible's limitations, to acknowledge that "the Bible does not address the full range of concerns that face today's Christian community. It is not always possible to find a satisfactory analogy (or other mode of relationship) between the Bible and to-day's concerns."[26]
- To be biblical is to continue the work of theological reconstruction that each new God-shaped hole requires.
- To be biblical is to risk new understandings of faith in a fragmented age.
- To be biblical is to be a visionary preacher.

The Bible canonizes a process of perpetually revising our theologies. The old-time religion of the Bible is continual new-time religion, a newness that does not ignore the past but listens to the cloud and the wind that are forever returning with their wisdom and tears, testifying that faith in God does not mean protecting the neatly inter-related hierarchies but opening truth to the soul.

The Bible also records how dangerous this work is. Challenging the hierarchies awakens resistance: the prophets are stoned, Jesus is crucified, visionary preachers are silenced for heresy.

THE GLORY OF THE CHRISTIAN RELIGION

The voices of Isaiah and the members of John's community call out from the cloud through the

God-shaped hole of our own age. They join with the voices of all the others who followed them to affirm what Tomasso Campanella bravely declared in defending Galileo against the charges of a fearful church: open inquiry is "an essential part of the glory of the Christian religion."

The cloud looks down through our God-shaped hole and asks: will our preaching participate in that glory? Or will our sermons constrict the human imagination, rushing in to plug up the God-shaped hole and shutting off the multiplicity of holy meanings that sound from the cloud and sing on the wind?

We have already seen that the eagerness to protect the neatly inter-related hierarchies has been a powerful force in the history of faith. And there is no reason to conclude that it is any weaker in our own age. A firestorm of protest followed the 1993 Re-Imagining Conference, a global theological colloquium considering new images and understandings of God, humanity, and church in light of women's experience. One participant wrote afterwards:

> Re-Imagining!
> How could such great adventure
> Become such sorrow![27]

Theological reconstruction is treacherous and tangled. It brings sorrow because it involves acknowledging the loss of things that we once held sacred and that others may still hold to be so.

Although we need to deal patiently with those who grieve a lost past, the cloud and the wind teach us that sorrow cannot deter us from facing up to the God-shaped hole. For example, while false prophets and diviners fed the exiles' illusions of a speedy return to Israel, Jeremiah helped them come to terms with reality. It was not God but their image of God that had collapsed with the temple. Rather than encourage their discredited theology, Jeremiah exhorted them to settle down to their new life in Babylon: "Build houses and live in them; plant gardens and eat what they produce . . . seek the welfare of the city where I have sent you into exile, and pray to the LORD on its behalf, for in its welfare you will find your welfare" (Jeremiah 29:5, 7).

Visionary preachers are no more called to encourage grief for the loss of an inadequate theology than was Jeremiah. Instead, the wind howls through the God-shaped hole to remind us of the reality greater than all our projected meanings. Listening to the wind, feeling the wind, breathing the wind, I realize in my being the truth of Rudolf Bohren's observation:

> Before there were written texts, there was the Spirit brooding over the waters until a voice spoke. When texts appeared, there came along with them books and libraries, universities and faculties, and a monstrous scholarly apparatus was installed in order to give texts a voice to carry the Spirit.[28]

Perhaps now it is time to reverse the process, to give the Spirit a voice to carry the texts, to return to the originating order so that the church, human life, the world can be re-created: first the wind upon the water, then the word that cleaves the dark with light (Genesis 1:1-3).

We breathe approximately ten million times as newborn living creatures before we speak our first words as children. Air filling and leaving our lungs is telling a truth never fully caught in the net of language. The primacy of breath reminds us of the primacy of Spirit, and suggests that the task of preaching while the church is under reconstruction begins with the confession that "we have a strong method to serve the letter, but we have not done enough to serve the Spirit theoretically, practically, and methodologically. This could only happen because we forgot that the Holy Spirit is also dedicated to us."[29]

When I survey the books upon my shelves, the full force of this confession falls upon my heart. I, like most preachers, have gathered volume upon volume of words about words, and I am sometimes tempted to believe Sunday's sermon rests in the tomes that line the shelves of my study. Such monumental verbosity results in "a dangerously artificial religion memorably described by the late Edwin Muir in his poem, 'The Incarnate One' as 'The Word made word.' "[30] Is there any way out of this predicament for preachers since preaching is by its very nature an art of words?

Yes, there is.

For some ways of employing language constrict the breathing of the Spirit far less than others. They bring us to the boundary of human articulation, where we look over the edge of reality and sense the deep dear core of things from which all that is true and good flows. Jesus is a master of such language:

> He speaks in the evocative, twinkling, perplexing idiom of moral poetry, in parables, paradoxes, mysterious figures, epigrams, and piercing summations which can dissolve history in an instant; he is able to superinduce poetry in even his most thickheaded conversants (perhaps poets may be comforted to find that *poetry, apparently, is the idiom of the Kingdom*).[31]

At the word "poetry" the cloud breaks into multiple choruses as psalmists, choirs of angels, poets, and hymnists fill the church of the God-shaped hole with the gathered praise of centuries of worship that continues and amplifies the dance of pulsing atoms and stars. For a moment I turn from my word processor and listen to the unbroken stream of rhapsodic song that flows from the intermingling of Wind and cloud:

Let everything that breathes praise the Lord
Gloria in excelsis Deo
Holy holy holy
O gladsome light
Veni Creator Spiritus
I'm going to sing when the Spirit says sing
Agios O Theos, agios ischuros, agios athanatos,
    eleison hemas
Death be not proud
Christ the Lord is risen today
Heleluyan heleluyan hele heleluyan
Immortal invisible God only wise
O for a thousand tongues to sing
Nobody knows the trouble I've seen Glory
    Hallelujah
Halle halle halle halleluyah . . .

Attending to the cloud, I become disoriented because "listening to great music is a shattering experience, throwing the soul into an encounter with an aspect of reality to which the mind can never relate itself adequately. Such experiences undermine conceit and complacency and may even induce a sense of contrition and a readiness for repentance."[32] Reeling from the music of the cloud, I find myself in a state of speechless confession. The music fades, I keep silence, and there appears in the cloud Tukaram, an Indian peasant mystic (1608–49), who articulates in a few lines addressed to God what the music of the ages has conveyed to my heart:

To tell the splendour of Thy love!

I sing, and sing,
Yet all the while the truth evadeth telling:

No words there are, no words,
To show Thee as Thou art.[33]

Tukaram's prayer and the cloud's multiple choirs draw me more deeply into the presence of the Spirit. The Spirit then redirects me from prayer to reflection. The Spirit enables my analytical reason to name what has gripped me with inarticulate wonder.

SPIRITUAL EXEGESIS

The interpreters of scripture who can most help us to fill the role of visionary preaching while the church is under reconstruction are those "who have been given part of the very same Spirit that blows through the biblical books."[34] Bohren, drawing upon the work of Peter Stuhlmacher, names such interpretation "Spiritual Exegesis and the Participation of the Spirit."[35] When I listen to the Wind and the cloud, I realize that "spiritual exegesis" describes what the church's poets have done through the ages. I mean by "poets" all who are gifted in the perception and expression of the Spirit. Out of the depths of belief and doubt, they produced hymns, spirituals, poems, sermons, the embroideries of legend and tradition, music, visual and dramatic art. They were visionary preachers to the broken worlds of their own times. They can instruct us in how to preach to a fragmented age. They provide models of spiritual exegesis for the church under reconstruction. They are a counterforce against repressive and destructive preaching from the Bible. Their work challenges

> today's new dogmatism[, which] is due to an insufficient teaching about the Holy Spirit and due, therefore, to the failure to discern the difference between the Spirit and the letter, to an insufficient reflection of the humanity of the Spirit. We stress the divinity of the Spirit and do not see how closely it is related to the flesh.[36]

The Spirit is related to the flesh through the workings of the imagination. Common speech acknowledges this relationship: creative work is "inspired," which means "in-spirited." The Bible provides a striking image that has fed this meaning of inspiration through the ages: we become living creatures when God breathes into our nostrils (Genesis 2:7).

Despite the close etymological linkage of "inspired" and "Spirit," there is a fear on the part of many religious people that creative imagination is unreliable and antithetical to faith. These believers have helped to create "one of the world's sorest bruises: the incompatibility between revelation and imagination, or in political terms, totalitarianism and liberalism."[37] For them revelation and imagination are polar opposites. They are like Captain Robert de Baudricout in George Bernard Shaw's play *Saint Joan.* He is confounded by the visionary preaching of Joan of Arc, as is the entire patriarchal church. In a sharp exchange, Joan rejects the simplistic dichotomy drawn by Robert and his ilk who masquerade their anxiety about her imaginative powers as a desire to protect the truth:

> JOAN. I hear voices telling me what to do. They come from God.
>
> ROBERT. They come from your imagination.
>
> JOAN. Of course. That is how the messages of God come to us.[38]

The visionary preachers who composed hymns, wrote lyrical verse, created legends, sculpted, and painted while the church was under reconstruction in their ages trusted that God communicated through their imaginations. They were in-spirited by the same Breath, the same Wind that moves through the God-shaped hole in our dome of meaning.

Though we would die without it, the breathwind-spirit[39] frightens us. We preachers fear the loss of exegetical precision and the illusion of control that it feeds. Perhaps we would be less fearful if we asked of our sermons what David Rosenberg asks of biblical translations: "What is less in error, a leaden cliché in place of the vibrant, ancient image, or an energetic, contemporary image that parallels the original Hebrew?"[40]

IMAGINATIVE ACCURACY

A poet aims for imaginative accuracy,[41] and imaginative accuracy is the goal of visionary preaching. We usually associate "accuracy" with measurable quantities. The recipe calls for three quarters of a cup of flour, the new shelf has to fit between the windows that are twenty-three and five-eighths inches apart. But how can the imagination be accurate? By its very character imagination seems to eschew accuracy. The difficulty arises from misunderstandings of the word "imagination." Although we sometimes let our imagination "run wild," creating a sermon involves disciplining our imaginings. Imaginative accuracy requires language that is congruent with what is felt, dreamed, and believed in the heart. Imaginative accuracy crystallizes our inchoate yearnings into forms that make those yearnings more accessible to us. We respond to a sermon that is imaginatively accurate with gratitude, because the dim flame that had been struggling to stay lit in our hearts now shines more brightly.

To understand imaginative accuracy listen again to the cloud. Consider, for example, the visionary preacher/poets who wrote the carols and hymns of Christmas, and observe how they amplify the spare accounts that Matthew and Luke offer us about

Christ's nativity. It is not the Scriptures but the poets who with imaginative accuracy tell us

that the angels touched "harps of gold,"

that the baby "no crying he makes,"

that "The Friendly Beasts" told what each gave,

that "snow had fallen, snow on snow,"

that Bethlehem enjoyed a "deep and dreamless sleep,"

that a woman by the name of "Jeanette Isabella" brought a torch,

that in the stable "all is calm, all is bright."

Not a single one of these details is in the Bible. But they are profoundly biblical in spirit, and they give expression to the wonder, the gratitude, the devotion that Jesus' birth awakens in us. They are imaginatively accurate versions of the nativity story.

IN THE BLEAK MIDWINTER

The creators of the carols continued the dynamic process that the biblical writers began. The scriptural stories of the nativity are not historical records but the fictions of the evangelists expressing the significance of Christ's birth. Listening to the cloud, I hear Matthew and Luke exchanging delighted comments with the carolers about one another's versions of the nativity. I sing Christina Rossetti's "In the Bleak Midwinter" and hear the evangelists marveling at how perfectly she grasped the meaning of magi and shepherd:

> What can I give Him,
> Poor as I am?
> If I were a shepherd
> I would bring a lamb,
> If I were a Wise Man
> I would do my part,—
> Yet what I can I give Him,
> Give my heart.[42]

Christina Rossetti wrote these words twelve years after Charles Darwin's *On the Origin of Species* (1859). It would be difficult to exaggerate the impact of his book upon western culture in general as well as the church specifically: "the reverberation of his ideas can be seen throughout the literature of the second half of the 19th century."[43] The theory of evolution ripped an enormous God-shaped hole in the roof of the Victorian church. A night of doubt had descended upon many thoughtful believers by the time Rossetti wrote her famous carol in 1871. In addition to the burden of Darwin's impact, the poet struggled with depression. She often felt her vital energies to be frozen and immobile. Living amidst the shadows of doubt and depression, she opened her carol

> In the bleak midwinter
> Frosty wind made moan,
> Earth stood hard as iron,
> Water like a stone;
> Snow had fallen, snow on snow,
> Snow on snow,
> In the bleak midwinter
> Long ago.

We would have no idea from this first stanza that the poem is "A Christmas Carol," except that is the title it bears. Rossetti is writing a new kind of carol. It does not start with singing angels or questing magi. A more confident faith can begin a carol with the rapture of the heavens, but such faith has been torn away by Darwin.

The "Long ago" of the first stanza's last line is a way of bringing perspective to the here and now, a vantage point for looking into the present bleak midwinter of post-Darwinian Christianity. The repeated "snow on snow, / Snow on snow" is less a description of the countryside around Bethlehem than the frozen, shadowed landscape of the heart that greets the incarnation. Rossetti has the theological courage of a visionary preacher to make the birth relevant to the bleak midwinter of her own age.

> Our God, Heaven cannot hold Him,
> Nor earth sustain;
> Heaven and earth shall flee away
> When He comes to reign:
> In the bleak midwinter
> A stable-place sufficed
> The Lord God Almighty
> Jesus Christ.
>
> Enough for Him, whom cherubim
> Worship night and day,
> A breastful of milk
> And a mangerful of hay;
> Enough for Him, whom angels
> Fall down before,
> The ox and ass and camel
> Which adore.

The birth of Christ does not thaw the frozen landscape. That will have to wait for when "Heaven and earth shall flee away, / When he comes to reign." Christ's birth does not bring spring but a companion for us who live "In the bleak midwinter." And if "A stable-place sufficed," and if it was "Enough" for Christ to have "A breastful of milk / And a mangerful of hay," then we who sing the carol can leave behind our ravenous hungers for a commanding certitude and find it "Enough" to receive the elemental simplicities that sustain life in a frozen world.

> Angels and archangels
> May have gathered there,
> Cherubim and seraphim
> Thronged the air,
> But only His mother
> In her maiden bliss
> Worshipped the Beloved
> With a kiss.

The heavenly host finally makes its entrance in this, the penultimate verse. But "Cherubim and seraphim" are not the most impressive thing about the scene. It is rather what happens "only" between the infant and the mother who "Worshipped the Beloved / With a kiss." Incarnation refocuses our energies on human relationships so that there is less need to mourn that Darwin has shaken the heavens. The birth of Christ has already redirected faith to consider the greater mystery of love.

The God-shaped hole of Christina Rossetti's age became for the poet an opportunity to find her way to a faith stripped of everything not essential: "Yet what I can I give him, / Give my heart." The poem is a visionary sermon, a spiritual exegesis, an imaginatively accurate reading of the birth narratives.

FIVE PRINCIPLES FOR VISIONARY PREACHING

Christina Rossetti models five principles for fulfilling the visionary role of preachers while the church is under reconstruction.

- Use the God-shaped hole to revitalize faith in God
- Draw upon the personal as a source of spiritual energy
- Employ the heart of tradition
- Visualize abstraction
- Discipline creativity with form

A large part of the power of Rossetti's carol derives from the opening verse, which so perfectly expresses the frozen landscape of post-Darwinian Christianity in Victorian England. If the frosty wind, the deep snows, and the frozen earth did not greet us at the start, if instead the carol opened with the second stanza, "Our God, Heaven cannot hold Him / Nor earth sustain," then it would be too facile in its piety. It would sound as if the church could preach the way it did before Darwin tore open the God-shaped hole in the dome of meaning. The carol would be like sermons that put congregations to sleep with the opening sentence: a cliché instead of an invitation to a dance. We are left sitting where we have always sat instead of moving more deeply into the mystery of God.[44] By facing up to the God-shaped hole in the first stanza, Rossetti wins a hearing for the stanzas that follow. The poet/preacher creates the possibility of revitalizing faith by reframing it with the current reality. The ability to express the culture's dilemma in such simple but profound language results in part from Rossetti's capacity to draw upon her own life as a spring of spiritual insight. The poet/preacher was familiar with depression. There is reason to believe that this had at least two sources: some form of sexual abuse by her father during childhood and the "well-attested tendency among female authors to sicken after publication."[45] Rossetti does not exhibit the secrets of her soul for us to gawk at, but she draws upon them to create poetry that resonates with the experience of others because it is so congruent with her own. She demonstrates how to handle one of the most difficult homiletical challenges: using the self without reducing truth to the limits of personal experience. While Rossetti is painfully aware of the God-shaped hole and the shadows that stalk her own life, she does not abandon tradition all together, but modifies it to match her personal experience as a woman. Thus, "neither in verse nor prose had she ever been able to address God the Father. It was always Christ whom she prayed to . . . a clear bias against paternal divinity is visible."[46] Unburdened of a father god, Rossetti is free to draw upon those portions of Christian tradition that do make sense of her experience. She holds together two seemingly unrelated realities: the beloved nativity stories and the experience of a post-Darwinian, sexually abused, Victorian poet, whose great talent was suspect because she was a woman. The tension between the two results in a carol/sermon of enduring power and beauty. As a visionary poet/preacher, she is able to use the incongruities of a fragmented age to create an imaginatively powerful witness to the meaning of Christ.

Christina Rossetti's poetry is a striking example of Paul Wilson's central metaphor for how a preacher's imagination works: creativity takes place in the spark gap between two realities that initially seem to be unrelated, just as a spark leaps between two differently charged wires held in proximity to each other.[47] The brilliance of the spark leaps to us through Rossetti's images. She does not have to offer long explanations because she employs the materiality of the world ("Earth stood hard as iron, / Water like a stone") and the onomatopoetic quality of language ("Frosty wind made *moan*") to reach to the nerve centers of our thought and feeling. This does not mean that image and narrative displace the need for a sharp homiletical point. Rossetti brings her sermon home with an evangelical affirmation: "Yet what I can I give Him, / Give my heart." The piety of the final stanza is traditional, but it strikes us with fresh force because the poet grounds her answer in the materiality of the world that has been pictured in the preceding stanzas. As a *vision*ary preacher she gives us a *vision* of what faith means.

Finally, Rossetti instructs preachers in the importance of form to discipline their creativity. The poem is a carol with a rhyme scheme and a hymnic meter (with slight variations). These are not small matters. They are crucial to the poem's effectiveness. The meter, rhyme, and simple diction, all characteristics of carols, remind us that we are participating in a great tradition of church song as we read or sing the poem. Rossetti understood what a poet of our generation would later write:

> There are, it seems, two Muses: the Muse of Inspiration, who gives us inarticulate visions and desires, and the Muse of Realization, who returns again and again to say, "It is yet more difficult than you thought." This is the muse of form . . . it may be that form, strictly kept, *enforces* freedom. . . . The mind that is not baffled is not employed. The impeded stream is the one that sings.[48]

Rossetti sings to us a carol/sermon that still haunts us because of the realism and beauty rung from her rigorously disciplined creativity. Her discipline is a reminder to all of us who preach that the muse of inspiration is not sufficient to create a sermon that will sing in the congregation's heart. We also need the muse of realization.

These, then, are five principles for achieving imaginative accuracy, for visionary preaching while the church is under reconstruction:

- Use the God-shaped hole to revitalize faith in God
- Draw upon the personal as a source of spiritual energy
- Employ the heart of tradition
- Visualize abstraction
- Discipline creativity with form.

When I shared these principles with a group of clergy, one preacher was particularly moved by the list and pointed out how each of these is characteristic of the finest African American preaching:

- the God-shaped hole has been the threat of meaninglessness created by racial oppression

- the use of the personal is reflected in giving one's witness during the sermon
- the heart of the tradition is seen in the recurring themes of Exodus and following Jesus
- visualization finds its way into eloquent picture painting and storytelling methods
- and the discipline of form is seen in communal expectations of being taken to the cross and lifted up out of sorrow.[49]

The clarity with which the preacher drew connections which had not occurred to me suggests a sixth principle for visionary preaching in a fragmented world: we need to test our imaginative accuracy within as diverse a community as possible.[50] There are interrelationships and insights that we will never know without the help of a multiplicity of perspectives.

THE HUMMINGS IN THE SOUL

Voices from the cloud begin to sing. Gustav Holst, whose musical setting of Rossetti's text can be found in most English language hymnals, is conducting. I join in singing and find myself no longer analyzing Rossetti's text. Instead, I am swept away by the deeper music which is manifest through the poetry and the melody yet is greater than either of them. It is the same music (listen for it in the spaces that follow the phrases below) that gathers us into its stream when we are moved

by a sermon

or a sacrament

or a work of art

or a word of kindness

or an act of justice

or a gesture of love

or a witness to faith

or an expression of grief

or a word of pardon

or a silence so deep that the silence is sound.

It is music but more than music.

It is poetry but more than poetry.

It is feeling but more than feeling.

It is thought but more than thought.

It is the groaning of creation.

It is the sighing of the Spirit.

It is all of these commingling in the heart.

Paul the apostle has described it with more imaginative accuracy than any other writer I have read: it is the Spirit interceding "with sighs too deep for words" because "we do not know how to pray as we ought" (Romans 8:26). Yet it is often through poetry and music that we become attentive to the "sighs too deep for words," which is exactly what is happening as I sing "In the bleak midwinter."

The music ends and I oscillate back from wonder to reflection, from image to idea, from visionary preaching to conceptual analysis. Burch Brown traces how this process of moving back and forth between poetic and reflective language has characterized western philosophy and theology:

> The mythic, symbolic, or parabolic language of scripture incites thinking that is of a nonsymbolic, conceptual, and literal order. I want to emphasize, however, that metaphors and symbols have the capacity to give rise to thought not only at the dawn of critical think-

ing but again and again throughout history and at various levels of understanding.[51]

I find that this historic process recapitulates itself in visionary preachers whenever they move back and forth between the poetic language of scripture, tradition, and worship and their efforts to make sense of that language in their sermons. Eugene Lowry considers this process to be essential to the vitality of preaching: "We ought to notice that the metaphoric tease has no tease at all without the discursive pole."[52] As a preacher I am constantly oscillating between the two. Even now words from Rossetti's carol keep interrupting my thought processes: "Earth stood hard as iron . . . Water like a stone . . ." I survey the church under reconstruction and I see that down through the God-shaped hole "Snow has fallen, snow on snow, / Snow on snow." The cold has settled in because theologians and pastors alike have been inattentive to the "sighs too deep for words." We have become enamored with the instrumentality of knowledge, whether it be how to write an article acceptable to the academy or how to organize a church for growth and success. Of course, we need such knowledge, but we also need to critique it: "Scholarly knowledge forgot how to worship a very long time ago. . . . It is bewitched and drunk with its own ideas, captured in its own constructions of the world and its agenda."[53] Visionary preaching in the church with the God-shaped hole begins with the invocation of the wind and the cloud, with song and prayer, with the poets who can help us tend anew to the "sighs too deep for words." As the Roman Catholic sister said upon first considering the God-shaped hole: "We do nothing immediately. We sit underneath the hole and wait."

> Through our fragmentary prayers
> and our silent, heart-hid sighs
> wordlessly the Spirit bears
> our profoundest needs and cries.

Deeper than the pulse's beat
is the Spirit's speechless groan
making human prayers complete
with the prayer that is God's own.

Let our jabberings give way
to the hummings in the soul
as we yield our lives this day
to the God who makes us whole.

Search and sound our mind and heart,
Breath and Flame and Wind and Dove,
let your prayer in us impart
strength to do the work of love.[54]

Our "jabberings" take primarily two forms. Sometimes they are the clichés of religious expression extracted from the Bible and tradition. Other times they are academic lingo, the words that dominate the theological conversation of one generation, then yield to a new set of terms in the next. In my own pilgrimage as a church member, seminary student, pastor, and professor I have traveled a winding road of different terms, each in its day looking as if it were the end point when it was in truth only one more bend along the way:

                    modernism

   neo-orthodoxy

                  ultimate concern

    authentic existence

relevance

       liberation

    discourse

    deconstruction

multiculturalism

    postmodernism

            what next?

Using specialized terms is not inherently bad or wrong. There is no escaping the need for theological jargon that facilitates intellectual debate or a language of piety that makes corporate worship possible. The problem arises when, divorced from any attentiveness to the movement of the Spirit, the language becomes hollow, becomes "jabberings." Jabberings do not communicate "strength to do the work of love." That requires something deeper: speech that draws from "the Spirit's speechless groan," from "the hummings in the soul."

I think of Martin Luther King Jr. and the power of his preaching. It was not just his eloquence, though he certainly was eloquent, but also the sound of his voice. In those resonant vibrations people heard a weeping and a singing, a sorrow and a hope that broke through to them. Even if they did not share King's Baptist faith, they heard through him the Spirit, and it empowered them to stand with him for the cause of justice.[55] In his preaching and life King let the "jabberings give way / to the hummings in the soul" so that he and his listeners received "strength to do the work of love."

Rather than patching the God-shaped hole with our "jabberings," we need to listen to the poets, to the voices from the cloud, and through them receive the wind of the Spirit. By "poets" I mean *all those with visionary gifts for perceiving and expressing the depths of the reality of God*. I sometimes call them "preacher/poets" because they proclaim the gospel to us through their art. Sometimes known to us by name, there are others who remain anonymous yet through sermon, song, prayer, legend, and other forms of art they made extraordinary contributions to the worship of the church while it was under reconstruction. Their historic witness gives us courage to face our own God-shaped hole:

A choice confronts us. Shall we, as we feel our foundations shaking, withdraw in anxiety and panic?
Frightened by the loss of our familiar mooring places,
shall we become paralyzed and cover our inaction with
apathy? If we do those things, we will have surrendered
our chance to participate in the forming of the future.[56]

The early church, bereft of Jesus' physical presence and disappointed in its hope for the imminent
establishment of the reign of God, might have acted
as Rollo May warns that we might, withdrawing "in
anxiety and panic." There is evidence in the
Scriptures to suggest that some believers did. But
others were bolder, sharing oral traditions, writing
gospels and letters, preaching unrecorded sermons, living the love of Christ, spreading their witness around the Mediterranean basin. Attentive to
the hummings in the soul, those early believers
became vessels of the Spirit. They were visionary
preachers. Long after they died, the faith they had
planted was to grow and spread in ways they never
foresaw.

Now it is our turn to carry on their tradition of
visionary preaching. We who minister beneath the
God-shaped hole turn to the preacher/poets in the
cloud in order to draw more faithfully upon "the
power at work within us" that "is able to accomplish
abundantly far more than all we can ask or imagine"
(Ephesians 3:20).

Chapter 2

The Spirit Sighs:
Search for the True Cross

THE LEGEND OF FINDING THE TRUE CROSS

The cloud drifts above the God-shaped hole, and on the wind I hear hymns about the cross, their phrases pouring out in one continuously connected childhood memory of church: "When I survey the wondrous cross on which the prince of glory died. . . . In the cross of Christ I glory, towering o'er the wrecks of time. . . . On a hill far away stood an old rugged cross, the emblem of suffering and shame. . . ." The music decrescendos and fades to spoken words about the cross that I have heard as often as the hymns:

"It is her cross to bear."

"God has given him a heavy cross."

"You just have to accept it: it's your cross."

The inflection in the voice suggests an inescapable fate: to fight back would be futile, it would be a rejection of God.

But the cross is also used to comfort, to bless, to give strength for the work of justice and love, and to "serve as a basic and inarticulate expression of religious sentiment on all sorts of occasions."[1] One symbol: multiple meanings and multiple effects.

The Spirit, not wanting us to reconstruct a church in which the central symbols of faith are misused, sighs: *search for the true cross.* I look up through the God-shaped hole wondering: How do I tell the true cross from a false cross?

Voices from the cloud remind the church under reconstruction that this is one of the perennial questions of Christian faith. For over a thousand years one of the most beloved stories of popular piety in Europe was "The Finding of the True Cross."

> The legend is first attested in Ambrose's funeral oration in honour of Theodosius the Great, some seventy years after Helena's death. [Helena was the mother of the Emperor Constantine.] The story spread rapidly from the end of the fourth century onwards. It became known not only in Greek and Latin, but also in Syriac, Coptic, Georgian, and several vernacular languages. Until deep into the Middle Ages the legend remained a very popular story which was also represented in the visual arts.[2]

If we are tempted to dismiss the tale for not being historically true, we need to remember that legends often throw open doors to the heart that factuality cannot even unlock. Legends, especially those that endure as long as this one, are imaginatively accurate about the yearnings, ideals and struggles of people. This story exemplifies what I described in the first chapter as the "poetry" of anonymous believers, the embroideries of legend and tradition that can instruct us in visionary preaching. They are a way to listen to the hummings of the soul, to the sighs of the Spirit giving expression to the prayers too deep for words. Just as Christina Rossetti's "In the Bleak Midwinter" reveals principles for preaching while the church is under reconstruction so too does the legend of finding the true cross.

Because it is a legend there is no single authoritative text. The story took multiple forms as the church adapted the earliest versions to new beliefs and experiences. Some of these developments, as we shall see, fed the worst of Christian bigotry. But in other cases, the evolving legend expressed the noblest intentions of Christians trying to be faithful to the meaning of the cross.

The mixed values of the legend make it all the more instructive for us who are seeking to be visionary preachers. For if a story that blends the best and worst in the human heart could be so important to believers for centuries, then it ought to sober our judgments of the sermons, prayers, rituals, and hymns that we create. We bring our own mixed hearts to the task, and the best and the worst in us will manifest itself in the church that we reconstruct. In the future we will look down from the cloud and not only be grateful that we had the privilege of giving witness to God, but we will also weep at our distortions. Reconstructing the church is never an occasion for arrogance, for mocking the limitations of our ancestors while touting how much better we understand the meaning of faith, justice, love, and grace. We are as mired in finitude as any of our predecessors.

The heroine of "The Finding of the True Cross" is an actual historical figure: Helena (c. 255–c. 330), mother of the Emperor Constantine. Although Helena's birth and origins are murky, she appears to have been a lower-class woman who might have been a stable worker or innkeeper. Ambrose said in praise of her: "Christ raised her from dung to power."[3] The concubine of Emperor Constantius

Chlorus, she was abandoned by him when political and social pressures made it expedient for him to marry Theodora. But when Constantine, Helena's son by Constantius, became emperor, her fortunes were reversed. She was elevated to a position of prominence as indicated by her title Helena *Augusta* and the many coins that were struck with her image.

In her old age Helena made a pilgrimage to the Holy Land, taking gifts to the churches that her son was building there as part of his Christianization of the empire. Helena's historical journey and the many acts of charity she performed along the way were the seeds that grew into the legend "The Finding of the True Cross."

JOURNEY TO THE CROSS

Tyrannius Rufinus (345–410), who recorded the most authoritative version we have of the legend, appears in the cloud. He explains that he got the story about Helena from Gelasius, Bishop of Caesarea,[4] who had written it down in Greek some time near the end of the fourth century. Rufinus translated it into Latin. Here is how it begins in English:

> At about the same time, Helena, the mother of Constantine, a woman of outstanding faith and deep piety, and also of exceptional munificence, whose off-spring indeed one would expect to be such a man as Constantine, was advised by divinely-sent visions to go to Jerusalem. There she was to make an enquiry among the inhabitants to find out the place where the sacred body of Christ had hung on the Cross. This spot was difficult to find, because the persecutors of old had set up a statue of Venus over it, so that if any Christian wanted to worship Christ in that place, he seemed to be worshipping Venus. For this reason, the place was not much frequented and had all but been forgotten. But when, as we related above, the pious lady hastened to the spot pointed out to her by a heavenly sign, she tore down all that was profane and polluted there. . . .[5]

55

When Rufinus gets this far into the story, he is interrupted by witnesses in the cloud who belonged to the church during the first three centuries, long before there ever was such a legend. The story baffles these believers because it was not until "following the Emperor Constantine's decrees of toleration and political recognition of Christianity [that] images of the Crucifixion began to enter into Christian art as the Cross, Crucifix, and Crucifixion became the central identifying emblems of the Christian, replacing that of the fish."[6]

"What?! A fish instead of the cross?" centuries of later believers shout in a single voice so loud that the remaining walls of the church with the God-shaped hole appear to totter. Scholars come to the defense of the early Christians and point out that the Greek word for "fish" was an acrostic whose letters were taken to stand for "Jesus Christ, God's son, savior." The fish was used as a "signifier of baptism, the Eucharist, the Last Supper, the Resurrection and immortality."[7] By way of contrast "The first known representation of Christ's crucifixion only dates from the first half of the fifth century and was depicted on an ivory relief of Italian workmanship."[8]

If we grew up in a church dominated by the cross in prayers, hymns, sermons, and architectural setting, we may shake our heads in disbelief. Our bewilderment is an occasion for seeing more deeply into the constructive nature of religious expression: the revelatory power of the cross was something that grew through time. "From Constantine's reign onwards, the Cross became increasingly prominent as a symbol until it eventually became the Christian symbol par excellence."[9]

The church was under reconstruction after Constantine accepted Christianity. It was being transformed from a marginal institution to one at the center of the culture. There was a need to interpret the meaning of Christ, his crucifixion and resurrection, in ways that would make sense to vast new numbers of believers. Although Paul and the evangelists had written about the cross and the crucifixion, their words alone were not adequate to establish its centrality to the life of faith. That depended on visionary, poetic preaching, the imaginative creativity we find in the legend of Helena's search.

The legend reminds us that finding the cross involves a journey. We who preach are not to assume that we or our congregations have already arrived at the true cross. In the church currently under reconstruction the meaning of the inherited symbols is no longer self-evident. Preachers cannot invoke the symbols and expect them automatically to awaken the depths of emotion and insight that they did in earlier generations. As Helena made a pilgrimage to Jerusalem, so we who preach beneath the God-shaped hole make a pilgrimage to find the meaning of the cross for our age.

It is not an easy journey. Helena finds that the cross is buried beneath a statue of Venus. She responds by tearing down "all that was profane and polluted there." For us who live under the God-shaped hole in a pluralistic society, this is one of the most troubling moments in the legend. Helena's destructive act appears to us an expression of religious absolutism. It fits with her son's policy of Christianizing the empire, and it typifies the religious absolutism that has extracted a massive and tragic cost from God's creation. Wars, hate crusades, inquisitions, and pogroms have resulted from the arrogance of rabid believers assuming that their faith was the only true faith and the others were "profane and polluted." For us who worship beneath the God-shaped hole, visionary preaching eschews the religious arrogance that destroys the human community: "It is this unrelenting argument within Christianity for its own uniqueness, i.e., for its own normative superiority over all other religions, that must be overcome in a pluralistic age, and in a pluralist pulpit."[10]

At these words, Helena herself appears above the God-shaped hole and quiets us with the observation that from the cloud she sees things that were invisible to the age of Constantine. The legend manifests the distortions of an imperial church, but its principle revelation still holds: there is a need to search for the true cross. If we will only hear her story to the end we will see how the cross can open Christians to a positive understanding of all people, even across the barriers of differing religious belief. The most faithful way of living in a pluralistic age is not to deny our tradition, but to consider how it opens us to the world of others. The best antidote for the abuse and distortion of the cross is not its abandonment. That will only leave it in the hands of those who continue to employ it for oppressive and prejudicial ends. The best antidote is to strip away the distortions of the cross in order to set free its restorative powers.

DEADLY DISTORTIONS OF THE CROSS

Helena motions to Rufinus to continue the legend.

Deep beneath the rubble she found three crosses lying in disorder. But the joy of finding this treasure was marred by the difficulty of distinguishing to whom each cross belonged. The board was there, it is true, on which Pilate had placed an inscription written in Greek, Latin and Hebrew characters. But not even this provided sufficient evidence to identify the Lord's Cross. In such an ambiguous case uncertainty requires

divine proof. It happened that in that same city, a certain prominent lady of that place lay mortally ill with
a serious disease. Macarius was at that time bishop of
the Church there. When he saw the doubts of the queen
and all present, he said: "Bring all three crosses which
have been found and God will now reveal to us which
is the cross which bore Christ." Then, together with the
queen and the others, he approached the sick woman,
went down on his knees and poured out the following
prayer: "Oh Lord, you saw fit through the Passion on
the Cross of your Only-begotten Son to grant salvation
to the human race, and now in our own time you have
inspired your handmaid to search everywhere for the
blessed wood on which our Saviour hung; now give us
a clear sign which of these crosses was made to glori-
fy our Lord and which were made to execute slaves. Let
this woman, now lying ill unto death, be recalled to life
from death's door as soon as the wood of salvation
touches her." His prayer finished, he first brought one
of the three crosses near, but nothing happened; then
he brought the second near—still no reaction.

Upon first hearing this part of the legend, many of
us Christians who are gathered beneath the God-
shaped hole are tempted to dismiss the tale as
primitive and magical. But from the cloud centuries
of believers protest the arrogance of our judging
their faith primitive and magical.

Helena suggests that we consider the depths that
lie beneath the surface of the narrative details. The
story reveals that one of the marks of a false cross
is that it leaves people in their brokenness. The sick
woman is not made whole by either of the false
crosses. And the same is true of us. There are crosses that do not heal or restore but that leave us to
die.[11] We who preach beneath the God-shaped hole
need to name these crosses. We need to describe
them and make sure that in the church under reconstruction our sermons and worship do not press
these crosses upon our congregations.

Perhaps the two most deadly distortions of the

cross are the cross of violence and the cross of passivity. We are familiar with the cross of violence. It is the burning cross of the Ku Klux Klan. It is the cross stamped on a brochure that proclaims: "Death to homosexuals." It is the warped cross featured on a poster from Germany in 1934: a row of male ministers in full clerical garb are lined up like soldiers, each carrying a cross on his shoulder as if it were a rifle. The horizontal beam of every cross has been twisted so that the top portion of each cross forms a swastika. To the left of this line of ministers is somebody identified as "Reichsbischof Müller," the bishop of the Third Reich. The bishop is reviewing the clergy as a general reviews his troops. Above the entire scene are the following words in bold German print: *The Reich Bishop Gets Christianity into Line.*[12]

I study this poster beneath the God-shaped hole and notice that the artist is John Heartfield. I repeat his name aloud, and he appears in the cloud and explains that his name was originally Helmut Herzfeld. He had been a soldier in World War I. When he got out of the service, he became so disgusted with the rise of Nazism in his country that he anglicized his name to John Heartfield. Since it was not an age when there was television and since political posters were a major way of shaping public opinion, Heartfield decided to run a counteroffensive against the Nazis. He made posters like this to protest against them.[13]

A few months before Heartfield drew this picture, the Third Reich had begun reconstructing the German church in three ways:

- The Nazis had called for the eradication of the Old Testament from the church's worship and reading.
- The nationwide church youth movement had been incorporated into Hitler Youth.

- The Reich Bishop had promulgated that congregations were not to talk about politically touchy subjects.

What the Nazis did is a warning to us about the repressive possibilities that are always waiting to be realized when the church is under reconstruction, when there is a time of social and theological instability. Nation and church joined together in distorting the gospel of Christ. They harnessed the energies of religion to demonize groups of people who were deemed unfit for the Third Reich, above all the Jews but also including gypsies and homosexuals. They warped the cross of Christ so that instead of expressing grace and love it stood for judgment and hate.

At the conclusion of Heartfield's testimony, Helena appears again in the cloud. This time she is weeping while a scholar beneath the God-shaped hole explains that for fifteen centuries prior to the Nazis anti-Judaism infected Christianity. Although the original version of Helena's story was "not characterized by any sort of anti-Judaism . . . anti-Judaism soon crept into the legend."[14] Helena sobs as the scholar recounts how her good name and the cross of Christ were dragged into the service of evil. In a fifth-century version of the legend as recorded by Judas Cyriacus,

Helena, the representative of Christianity, accuses the Jews of deliberately hiding the Cross, by which their faith would be defeated if it were found. The Cross, which the Jews had hoped to use as an instrument to extinguish Christianity, became the symbol of their own defeat. In the Judas Cyriacus legend Helena's speeches reflect the opinion of Christian theologians about Judaism. Like Ambrose, Jerome and Chrysostom, Helena accuses the Jews of being blind for not understanding their own prophets, of having killed Christ, and of being deserted by God for not recognizing Christ as the Messiah. The legend therefore fits perfectly into the climate of anti-Judaism at the beginning of the fifth century.

61

It was in all likelihood because of its anti-Jewish character that the legend featuring Judas Cyriacus ousted the
original legend of Helena, at least in the West, and
became in the Middle Ages the most popular version of
the legend of the discovery of the Cross.[15]

As Helena weeps, nearly the entire cloud joins her:
How did we ever let this happen? How did we turn the
cross of Christ into a symbol of hatred and prejudice?
The magnitude of the terror brought on by the
distorted use of the cross begins to dawn upon us
who want to reconstruct the church with the God-
shaped hole. Perhaps we ought to leave the hole
there and not try to fill it with anything. Let it be an
eternal reminder that our faith is in God and not in
our projected meanings that we keep distorting in
order to claim divine sanction for behavior based
on fear. But as we think this, the cloud calls out:

Open truth to the soul.
Open truth to the soul.

Abandoning the cross will not help us open truth to
the soul. It will only leave the cross in the hands of
those who want to use it to reinforce the hierarchies of power and hatred.
Through her tears Helena reminds us that we
have only looked at one of the three crosses. When
the second cross is brought near the sick woman in
the legend there is still no reaction. The cross of violence is not the only false cross. There is also the
cross of passivity. This is a much harder cross to
picture. We do not have the unforgettable images of
burning crosses and crosses warped into swastikas.
Yet the cross of passivity is in some ways the
more insidious because it can so easily be dressed
up in the guise of piety and devotion. Giving in to
despair over injustice or abuse, we say to ourselves

and to others: "It is our cross to bear." But this distorts Christ's teaching as presented in the Gospels. Jesus says: "If any want to become my followers, let them deny themselves and take up their cross and follow me" (Matthew 16:24). Jesus does not command us to take up the cross. He leaves it to us to decide: if we want to follow him. We are not passive recipients of a cross that is forced upon us.

Using the cross to debilitate the struggle against injustice is a misuse of the cross: "to resign ourselves to what others tell us is our lot and to accept suffering and self-effacement is not a virtue."[16] The passive cross can be as deadly as the violent cross. It does not bring the swift death of persecution, but it brings the long, lethal decay of failing to employ the gifts of rebellion and change that God has given us. The passive cross, the cross of imposed sacrifice

> not only masks the violence and horror of human suffering, but serves also to justify its existence and continuation. It is naïve and irresponsible for theologians and preachers to think that this kind of proclaimed theology does not substantially encourage thousands of people in the United States to fail to respond to suffering in their own country and around the world.[17]

Helena listens to these words, wipes her tears, and reminds us that this is why we need to search for the true cross and to test what kind of cross we are preaching. If it leaves people as broken and wasted as the woman in the legend after she touches the first two crosses, then it is not the cross of Jesus Christ.

THE RESTORATIVE POWERS
OF THE TRUE CROSS

The witnesses in the cloud weep at the distorted ways they used the cross on earth. The wind carries their weeping into the church under reconstruction and into our hearts. Their sorrow mixes with ours and with the sighs of the Spirit, with the prayers too deep for words, until we yearn with our whole being for the revelation of the true cross. Helena motions to Rufinus to continue the Legend, and he resumes:

> But when [Bishop Macarius] brought the third cross near, the woman suddenly opened her eyes and got up, all her strength restored. She ran through the house more quickly than when she had been well, and began to praise the power of the Lord.

Finding the true cross makes the woman a new person, possessing more life than she had before her illness. Her healing is a sermon about distinguishing the true cross from the false cross. The false cross is the cross of death. It leaves us dead in our sin whether our sin is the arrogance that leads to violence or the passivity that ends in fatalism. The true cross is the cross of life, restoration, wholeness, vitality, new being.

THE FORGOTTEN PRAYER FROM THE CROSS

What gives the true cross these restorative powers? The wind blows through the God-shaped hole and brings back to us the stories of the cross that predate the legend, the passion accounts of the evangelists Matthew, Mark, Luke, and John. These are not eyewitness reports but, like the legend, attempts to express the character of the love that seeks to transform our broken lives, the love that flows through Jesus Christ.

It is a love that liberates those who suffer to acknowledge their abandonment and desperation. At the true cross there is a confrontation with God for God's failure to act. At the true cross we hear Christ cry: "My God, my God, why have you forsaken me?" (Matthew 27:46; Mark 15:34). The words are taken from Psalm 22, one of the great laments in the Bible. Lament is the forgotten prayer from the cross, or if not forgotten, then reinterpreted to soften Christ's desperation: we comfort ourselves by noting that Psalm 22 ends in praise and hope, and by speculating that its opening verse on Jesus' lips is meant to invoke the whole psalm.

But the Spirit sighs against our desire to concoct a theology that lessens or justifies the horror of what happened. An innocent man, betrayed by one of his followers and abandoned by the rest, was tortured and executed: "My God, my God, why have you forsaken me?"

The Spirit sighs that we are not to silence the cries of the desperate. We are not to mangle the prayer of the heart with a theology born of our unwillingness to face the brute facts of cruel and unjust suffering. The Spirit sighs on behalf of all the countless human beings who feel abandoned beneath a silent heaven:

> The death of Jesus testifies that God shares even in the cataclysmic moment every person confronts in death. God is present in the days that have been granted to persons on this earth; God is also present in the day when death brings experience on this earth to a decisive end. Because Jesus himself went through the experience of death, our experience of death does not separate us from him.[18]

The Spirit sighs on behalf of a woman I once visited in the hospital. Over the years she had undergone multiple procedures to correct a congenital condition. Now she was facing still another painful operation. I asked before I left if she, an active life-time church member, would like me to pray with her. She said "No." She had prayed and prayed and nothing had ever come of it. I then asked if I might read some-

65

thing from the Bible, and she answered, "Yes, but make it brief." I opened my pocket Bible and read:

> How long, O Lord? Wilt thou forget me for ever?
> How long wilt thou hide thy face from me?
> How long must I bear pain in my soul,
> and have sorrow in my heart all the day?
> (Psalm 13:1-2a RSV)

She responded in astonishment: "That's in the Bible?" I told her that it was there so that people for all time would know that when they felt abandoned by God, they could let God have it. They could pray with the full, fierce anger of someone abandoned.

She asked if I might mark the psalm and leave the Bible with her. I did, promising to come back in the morning just before her operation. When I returned, the Bible was open on her lap and she told me she had been praying the psalm all night.

The Spirit sighs through this story. The Spirit sighs against happy-time religion that buries the true cross, the cross that liberates those who suffer to acknowledge their abandonment and desperation. The Spirit sighs to bring back the forgotten prayer from the cross. Here was a woman who had gone to church all her life and had undoubtedly heard scores of sermons about the cross. But when she most needed the real cross, the cross that would liberate her lament, she did not even know about it.

The woman is not alone. Her tribe is legion, and I fear it is growing from a concern that I have heard repeated again and again by musicians and pastors. They tell of church growth literature that claims worship leaders should never choose music in a minor key. It is happy up-beat music in a major key that attracts people. But what about the woman who feels abandoned by God? What about the people who need to weep and lament? What about the necessity of the minor key to the gospel? What about those who ache to gather at the true cross, the cross from which Christ cries "My God, my God, why have you forsaken me?"

WERE YOU THERE WHEN THEY CRUCIFIED MY LORD

Perusing my collection of denominational hymnals, I do not find a single index that has an entry for "lament." There is adoration, praise, thanks, forgiveness, and so forth, but not one entry for lament. Although lament is a major form of prayer in the Bible, it is noticeably lacking from most of our liturgies.

Nevertheless, lament has not completely disappeared. It persists among those who have suffered and been abandoned. They know the power of lament even if they have not called it by that name. The Spirit has sighed through them and the true cross has been revealed in their song and poetry:

Were you there when they crucified my Lord?
(were you there)
Were you there when they crucified my Lord?
(were you there)
Oh! Sometimes it causes me to tremble, tremble, tremble.
Were you there when they crucified my Lord?
(were you there)

Were you there when they nailed him to the tree?
(were you there)
Were you there when they nailed him to the tree?
(were you there)
Oh! Sometimes it causes me to tremble, tremble, tremble.
Were you there when they nailed him to the tree?
(were you there)

Were you there when they pierced him in the side?
(were you there)
Were you there when they pierced him in the side?

67

(were you there)
Oh! Sometimes it causes me to tremble, tremble, tremble.
Were you there when they pierced him in the side?
(were you there)

Were you there when the sun refused to shine?
(were you there)
Were you there when the sun refused to shine?
(were you there)
Oh! Sometimes it causes me to tremble, tremble, tremble.
Were you there when the sun refused to shine?
(were you there)

Were you there when they laid him in the tomb?
(were you there)
Were you there when they laid him in the tomb?
(were you there)
Oh! Sometimes it causes me to tremble, tremble, tremble.
Were you there when they laid him in the tomb?
(were you there)

The singer/poet, unknown to us yet known to God, has found the true cross. The singer/poet makes no attempt to sweep away the terror of what has happened to Jesus. There is not the slightest appeal to a theological rationalization that would lessen the brutal, sad reality.

The sorrow of the heart is communicated by the slurred musical phrase which carries the interjection "Oh!" and the held note on the second syllable of "tremble," repeated three times. The prosody of congregational song in English usually highlights the accentual pattern of the language. But in this spiritual, placing the held note on the unaccented syllable of the word destabilizes the meter to create the affect of trembling. The music makes the meaning of the word sonically manifest.

The spiritual is an imaginatively accurate reading of the crucifixion as a reality fully present in the experience of the singer/poet. The intensity of personal engagement is revealed in the way Jesus is named in the first stanza: "my Lord." As a slave, the singer/poet was forced day by day to obey an earthly lord: the slave master. In acknowledging Jesus as "my Lord" the singer/poet asserts that in the ultimate scheme of things the subservience of the slave to the master has no standing. "My Lord" is Jesus, not "Mas'sa."

The singer/poet trembles at the depth of "my Lord's" identification with the suffering of the slaves. It is almost beyond belief that "my Lord" would endure suffering as great as the slaves. "Were you there?" Not just were you there at Calvary, but were you there with the suffering slaves? Do you know what we have been through? Do you know our crucifixion at the hands of our task masters? "My Lord" knows. "My Lord" has been crucified, nailed, pierced, and laid in a tomb. Were you there?

As the spiritual continues, we hear more weeping from the cloud. This time it is a preacher, who in his earthly life invoked a demonic biblicism and its accompanying authoritarian god to justify slavery:

> The only rule of judgment is the written word of God. The Church knows nothing of the intuitions of reason or the deductions of philosophy, except those repro- duced in the Sacred Canon. . . . She . . . has no right to utter a single syllable upon any subject except as the Lord puts words in her mouth. . . . Her creed is an authoritative testimony of God and not a speculation. . . . As long as that race [African Americans], in its com- parative degradation, coexists, side by side with the white, bondage is its normal condition.[19]

But for the singer/poet of the spiritual the slave master's image of a deity who is a rigid biblicist has collapsed. There is a God-shaped hole in the version of Christianity proclaimed by the owners to the slaves. The singer/poet reconstructs the church by offering an image of "my Lord" who suffers with the slaves.

"My Lord's" suffering inverts the usual order of things so that the world no longer operates in its established patterns: "Were you there when the sun refused to shine?" Although based on the scriptural description of the earth growing dark from noon until three when Christ was crucified (Luke 23:44), the singer/poet expands the biblical meaning with the strong verb *refused* to shine." The one thing that a slave could never do with impunity was refuse to obey the master. But in the inverted order of reality brought on by the suffering of "my Lord," obedience to the tyrannical order crumbles. If "the sun refused to shine," it opens up the possibility of refusal for the slaves. Christ is bringing in the day when they will "refuse" to obey their masters. Singing the spiritual, they taste liberation.

The singer/poet models how to find the true cross and use it in reconstructing the church. The singer/poet does not abandon the cross, for that would leave the symbol exclusively in the hands of the slave masters. A false cross would triumph, a cross that reinforces a theology of passive acceptance, a cross that encourages submission and subservience. The God-shaped hole would be filled in with images that suffocate the will to be free.

Instead the singer/poet takes the symbol and travels deeper and deeper into its meaning through the reality of the slaves' experience. The poet/singer finds the true cross and allows its liberating power to flow through the spiritual.

The singer/poet's bold theological work is a parable about preaching beneath the God-shaped hole in our own time. It demonstrates how to become visionary preachers in the church under reconstruction. We cannot afford to abandon the cross to believers who want to wield it as a club. The cross of violence is a lethal weapon in the hands of those who hate religious pluralism and who despise homosexuals, lesbians, artists who reach beyond the bounds of conventional taste, racial groups a society deems inferior, and families that do not conform to a particular pattern. We need the courage and imagination of the poet/singer who makes audible the humming of the soul in the presence of the true cross, who frees our lament in order to engage our energies to struggle for the liberation of all God's creatures.

THE LOCATION OF THE TRUE CROSS

Singing "Were You There" beneath the God-shaped hole, I look up and see in the cloud vast throngs of former slaves. Although spirituals were the creation of particular singer/poets, their work was fed by the experience of the entire community. The pathos and joy of their black brothers and sisters poured through their song.

The African American singer/poets were not unlike John the evangelist, whose community had a hand in the writing of his Gospel. The Muratorian Canon, an early listing of writings the church held sacred, describes the process:

> The fourth gospel is that of John, one of the disciples. . . . When his fellow-disciples and bishops exhorted him he said, "Fast with me for three days from today, and then let us relate to each other whatever may be revealed to each of us." On the same night it was revealed to Andrew, one of the apostles, that John should narrate all things in his own name *as they remembered them.*[20]

John's church was a community of shared memory, and that memory reached beyond the stories about Jesus to include the history of their life together. When John wrote that "one of the soldiers pierced [Christ's] side with a spear, and at once blood and water came out" (John 19:34), the words did more than take the community back to Calvary. It evoked in them the memory of all the times that they had shared the Eucharist and witnessed baptisms together.

Blood and water flowed with the memory of their hanging together as a group in the face of rejection and persecution. Blood and water preserved the memory of shared suffering and faith. Blood and water were the effusions of the tree around which they gathered.[21] Blood and water marked the location of the true cross in the midst of their community.

The throngs of liberated slaves and the members of John's community begin a litany in the cloud.

The liberated slaves sing:

Were you there when they pierced him in the side?
(were you there)
Were you there when they pierced him in the side?
(were you there)

The members of John's community answer:

Yes, we were there.
The water flowed
every time we celebrated a baptism.
The blood flowed
every time we shared the Eucharist,
every time our members suffered persecution and death.

Then all together in one voice:

Oh! Sometimes it causes me to tremble, tremble, tremble.
Were you there when they pierced him in the side?
Yes, we were there.

QUESTIONS VISIONARY PREACHERS ASK ABOUT THE CROSS

Years ago someone gave me a medical article that attempted to account for the flow of blood and water from the crucified Jesus on a purely physiological basis. As reasonable scientific speculation it might have been well founded, but as a piece of theology it was bankrupt. It depended upon a literalism that abrogates the imaginative accuracy of John's community and the liberated slaves. The true cross is the tree that grows among the community of the suffering.

Connecting blood and water, the symbols of communion and baptism, with the crucifixion of Jesus was an act of theological construction that bonded John's community to one another and to Christ. Their theological daring, like the African American spiritual, is a parable for us about how to be visionary preachers in a church under reconstruction. John's community did not travel back to Jerusalem. They made their pilgrimage to the cross where they lived. They made their pilgrimage every time they broke the bread and poured the wine, every time they welcomed a new disciple with the ritual sign of water in the name of God. Theirs was not an archaeological theology of the cross, an attempt to return to the originating event. Through their worship they fed on a living theology of the true cross, the tree that grows in the midst of a suffering community.

The cross of Christ, rooted in the joy and grief of a community, energizes the visionary preachers who minister to the church under reconstruction. Visionary preachers find inherited understandings of the cross less important than thinking creatively about the cross in the present. Although the past remains a source of wisdom, "archaeology is no substitute for theology. The question of historical actuality looms too large in the American mind and probably contributes to the misinterpretation of countless scriptural passages."[22]

As Oscar, a Nicaraguan peasant, puts the matter:

> Lots of people in Holy Week think only about the suf-
> ferings of Jesus, and they don't think about the suffer-
> ings of so many Christs, of millions of Christs that
> exist. And Jesus didn't want them to be wailing for him
> but to wail for the others that were going to suffer like
> him or worse than him.[23]

Instead of obsessing about the "historical actuality" of the true cross, visionary preachers adopt the
more faithful strategy used by Oscar and John's
community. Visionary preachers allow the cross
and their lives to interweave so that the meaning of
each is continuously adapted and expanded by the
other. Visionary preachers ask:

Where is the blood and water flowing in our community?

Where is the cross now?

Who is praying, "My God, my God why have you
abandoned me?"

By asking these pointed questions, visionary
preachers create God-shaped holes. They crumble
the symbols of conventional meaning that enforce
submission to the world's inequity and brutality:

> The historical process by which a nation, race or class
> become subjects [active participants in their destiny]
> almost always begins with their breaking through the
> power of the official idea of history by exposing it as
> propaganda on the part of those who rule them. . . .
> Peasants, for example, have revealed their memory of
> suffering in their chronicles and citizens have made
> that memory visible in their art. In this way they have
> derived the power to resist the threat to their identity.[24]

Blood and water empowered John's church "to resist
the threat to their identity." Surrounded by the imperial power of Rome, they could easily have dissolved
as a community, except that the memory of Christ's
death and the memory of all those with whom they
had shared the sacraments sustained them. Blood

and water flowed from the true cross that was planted in the midst of their corporate life. Blood and water reinforced the community's identity and gave it the strength to endure. Blood and water continue to flow in the church under reconstruction, and to confront us with the meaning of the cross for our age:

> How do I handle the three main goals all too many Americans admit to: money, power, fame? How do I relate to Christ crucified today—crucified in the children abused and the elderly unloved, in the AIDS-afflicted and the drug-addicted, in blacks still enslaved and Hispanics newly unwelcome, in the homeless and the hopeless in my own parish?[25]

TRUST IS NOT SUBMISSION

The cross that gives the church its enduring identity also awakens a trust in the source of all that is: "Father, into your hands I commend my spirit" (Luke 23:46). Luke alone ascribes these words to the dying Christ. They are taken from Psalm 31:5*a*, but there is one startling addition in the Gospel: "Father." Possibly an editorial modification by the evangelist, that lone word reveals more than Luke's understanding of Jesus' relationship to God. Although many of us in the church under reconstruction have difficulties with the "Father" language because "it has established a hegemony over the Western religious consciousness,"[26] the intimacy and depth of relationship suggested by the term in its original context are probably close in spirit to what we desire to express by inclusive language. In the community for which Luke wrote, calling God "Father" would have been a source of solace and peace. When believers were in distress they could find comfort in praying as Jesus did at the end: "Father, into your hands I commend my spirit."

However, for us who gather beneath the God-shaped hole, it is essential that we not pray this prayer prematurely. If we do, we will return to the cross of passivity. God does not want us to succumb to distortions of the cross while we cover our cowardice with piety.

- Trust is *not* submission.
- Trust is *not* accepting abuse and injustice.
- Trust is *not* caving in to conditions that God has given us strength to challenge and change.
- Trust *is* what feeds the courage of visionary preachers to deal with the God-shaped hole.
- Trust *is* the sign that we believe too deeply in God to spend our ministries patching up this fragmented age with old theological plaster that will never hold.
- Trust *is* releasing ourselves from the burden of doing anything more when we have done all we can.
- Trust *is* the opening of the heart to the confluence of gracious powers flowing from the deep dear core of things.
- Trust *is* confidence that the source of breath and pulse will not abandon us when breath and pulse cease.
- Trust *is* reaching our hand into the uncharted night and expecting another will grasp ours and lead us onward.
- Trust *is* giving up our last breath as our eternal prayer: "Mother/Father, into your hands I commend my spirit."

At these words, a round-faced pastor wearing wire-rimmed glasses appears in the cloud: Dietrich Bonhoeffer (1906–1945), the German pastor who was executed for his participation in a plot to kill Hitler and bring down the Third Reich. Helena calls to us through the God-shaped hole, and pointing to

Bonhoeffer, she explains that he lived out the meaning of finding the true cross. He was a visionary preacher in a church under reconstruction, and his life and witness can instruct us how to fill that visionary role for our own age.

LIVING THE MEANING OF THE TRUE CROSS

I open a book that depicts Bonhoeffer's life in pictures, the volume in which I discovered John Heartfield's poster of swastika-toting ministers. The book's first group of photographs features Bonhoeffer's grandparents and uncles. He came from an intellectually aristocratic family in Germany. One of his forebears was a nineteenth-century theologian who wrote the standard work that every seminary student studied in systematic theology. There were also distinguished physicians, people of science, and mathematicians.

Among the photographs of these turn-of-the-century people I see a picture of seven children. They are arranged like organ pipes, from the tallest to the shortest, and there is Dietrich, the next to the shortest. At his side is his twin sister, Sabine, with whom he continued to have a close relationship throughout his life.

There is another picture with just him and Sabine together at about age twelve. She holds his left arm and averts her gaze downward while he looks straight into the camera. It is a stylized romantic pose, obviously arranged by the photographer, but it cannot help touching the heart of the viewer.

I study all the pictures closely. I want to know what a visionary preacher looks like in childhood. I want to see if there is some hint in the eyes or the way he holds his body of the courage and faith he would show as an adult.

Helena calls from the cloud for me to keep going. I continue turning the pages of the picture book. And now I find the family photographs giving way to mobs saluting Der Führer. Bonhoeffer immediately saw the danger that Adolf Hitler represented. Hitler was made Chancellor on January 30, 1933, and only two days later Bonhoeffer during a radio broadcast "warned against the possibility of Germany slipping into an idolatrous cult of the *Führer* (leader) who could very well turn out to be a *Verführer* (misleader) and one who mocks God himself."[27] As soon as Bonhoeffer began his critical remarks, he was cut off the air. It was possibly the first governmental action of the Third Reich against free speech.

Bonhoeffer's warning about slipping into an idolatrous cult of the Führer proved on target. One school catechism of the Third Reich affirms: "as Jesus set men free from sin and hell, so Hitler rescued the German people from destruction. . . . Jesus built for heaven; Hitler, for the German earth" (p. 110). The words of the catechism confirmed what Bonhoeffer, drawing upon the work of Martin Luther, once told Karl Barth: "the curses of the godless sometimes sound better in God's ear than the hallelujahs of the pious" (p. 12). Even though he was a man of profound religious faith, as a visionary preacher Bonhoeffer was not fooled by piety. He saw how easily religion is bent out of shape and fused with political power for evil purposes.

Bonhoeffer did not reject all forms of piety. He was a man of prayer, and when he organized his own seminary to provide an alternative to the theological schools of the state church, he made prayer a part of the curriculum. His biographer, Eberhard Bethge recalls: "Into these prayers he would put his will, his understanding and his heart" (p. 27).

After several pages of photographs of Nazi rallies

in the Bonhoeffer picture book, I come again upon the John Heartfield poster "Getting Christianity into Line." Bonhoeffer refused to get Christianity into line. He rejected the false cross of anti-Jewish violence and the false cross of the passivity of the clergy who did nothing to protest the terror. When the Nazis organized people to smash the windows of Jewish houses and stores and to burn synagogues during the notorious Kristallnacht of November 9, 1938, Bonhoeffer was enraged both by that horrible action and by the pious silence of the clergy. Bonhoeffer spoke vehemently against the religious rationale that was invoked to justify the violence: namely, the claim that the Jews deserved such treatment because they were cursed for the death of Jesus.

Bonhoeffer's courage was nurtured by the example of his grandmother, Julie Tafel Bonhoeffer, who herself bravely resisted the Nazi tactics of terrorism against the Jews. One day when the S.S. troops and Hitler Youth were picketing a Jewish shop, Julie Tafel Bonhoeffer, by then in her nineties, walked right through the picketers into the store to make her usual purchases. She embodied another of Bonhoeffer's religious principles: "Confession of faith is not to be confused with professing a religion. . . . The primary confession of the Christian before the world is the deed which interprets itself" (p. 86). That was what impressed Dietrich with his grandmother: her deeds interpreted themselves.

From the cloud Helena explains it is also the quality that impresses her with Brother Dietrich: the deed of his life interprets itself. His actions as a visionary preacher make clear that he found the true cross and bore it to the end of his life.

Such a life arises from more than sheer self-will. His admiration for his courageous grandmother reveals that there were deep strains of decency in his family that were a formative influence upon him, something which he openly acknowledges in these words from the sermon he preached at his grandmother's funeral, January 15, 1936:

> She lived to be ninety-three years old, and imparted to us the legacy of another era. For us, a world comes to an end with her, a world which we all somehow bear and want to bear within us. Right that does not compromise, free speech of a free person, the binding character of a word once given, clarity and plainness of speech, integrity and simplicity in private and public life—to this she was devoted with her whole heart. It was her life. In her life, she came to know that it costs toil and trouble to accomplish these ideals in one's own life. She did not avoid this toil and trouble. She couldn't bear to see these ideals disregarded, to see a person's right violated. That is why her last years were clouded by the great sorrow that she bore on account of the fate of the Jews in our nation. (p. 270)

The words which Dietrich Bonhoeffer spoke about his grandmother can now be applied with equal appropriateness to him.

His observations about the cost of such a life find their echo in his theological writings, especially in one of his most famous passages, the opening to his book *The Cost of Discipleship.* Whether or not Bonhoeffer had his grandmother in mind when he wrote these words, it is not far-fetched to think that his theology was fed by the example of her integrity:

> Cheap grace is the deadly enemy of our Church. We are fighting today for costly grace. Cheap grace means grace sold on the market like cheapjacks' wares. . . . Cheap grace is the preaching of forgiveness without requiring repentance, baptism without church discipline, Communion without confession, absolution without personal confession. Costly grace . . . is costly because it costs a man his life, and it is grace because it gives a man the only true life. [28]

The strenuousness of Bonhoeffer's theological insights, the way he refused to let religion give him a rosy-colored view of life, resulted in his being highly responsive to the actuality of the world's situation. But many other Christians found themselves unable to confront reality so boldly.

The editors of Bonhoeffer's essential writings observe how

> In his letter of October 24, 1936, Bonhoeffer dismisses with mild contempt the flocking of some mainstream people to attractive groups, which were springing up within Germany and elsewhere, attracting people by their appeal for personal conversion, promise of devotional fulfillment, and offer of a nonpolitical, nonthreatening way of being a church. He cautions against surrendering to the lure of such groups because, for him, such a surrender meant being less a mainstream church with critical power in the state and being more a fringe church unable to preach the gospel to the state. (pp. 409-10)

At these words Helena cannot contain herself. She points out that "surrendering to the lure" of these groups constitutes surrendering to the false cross of passivity. The seeming innocence of religious group intimacy becomes an instrument of corrosion, sapping people's energies for engaging the necessary political and social struggles of their time.

Bonhoeffer became so disillusioned with the church's unwillingness to confront and fight the evil of Nazism that there was a period during 1933–1934 when he wanted to go to India and study with Gandhi, hoping that he might find guidance there in how to carry on the struggle in Germany. He writes to his grandmother in May of 1934:

> Lately I have been occupied very intensively with questions relating to India and believe that one can perhaps learn a great deal there. In any case, it sometimes seems to me as if in their brand of "paganism" there is placed more Christianity than in our whole Reich Church. Of course, Christianity did indeed come from the East originally, and we have Westernized it in such a way and permeated it with merely civilized consid-

erations that, as we now see it, it is almost lost to us.
Unfortunately I have hardly any confidence left in the
church opposition. (p. 420)

As one who had found the true cross, Dietrich
Bonhoeffer knew that wisdom comes in many
forms and bears many names. The true cross is the
cross that marks the end of Christian triumphalism
and Christian exclusivism. For a visionary preacher
the true cross "opens truth to the soul" wherever
that truth is revealed and whatever religious or
nonreligious label it bears.

Bonhoeffer never ended up going to India.
However, he did everything possible to provide
some form of organized Christian opposition to the
Nazis, including his active work in what was called
"The Confessing Church," a movement of about one
quarter of the German pastors who resisted the distortions of the established Reich church, especially
its support of Hitler and his anti-Jewish policies.

As part of that movement Bonhoeffer partic-
ipated in opening an alternative seminary in 1935
that was located in Finkenwalde, near Stettin, in
Pomerania. The school lasted only until September,
1937, when it was closed by the Gestapo, the
secret police of the Nazis.

Then in April, 1938, the established church insti-
tuted for its ministers an oath of allegiance to Hitler:

> Anyone who is called to a spiritual office is to affirm
> his loyal duty with the following oath: "I swear that I
> will be faithful and obedient to Adolf Hitler, the *Führer*
> of the German Reich and people, that I will conscien-
> tiously observe the laws and carry out the duties of my
> office, so help me God." . . . Anyone who refuses to
> take the oath of allegiance is to be dismissed. (p. 461)

John Heartfield points down from the cloud at
his poster "Getting Christianity into Line," which

features the clergy toting the swastika-shaped crosses. The apostasy Heartfield had pictured four years earlier was now fully realized in the clerical oath of loyalty to the Führer. Helena exclaims yet again that this is why the search for the true cross is essential. Without a critical understanding of the cross, its meaning will be warped and its religious power harnessed for the worst ends.

As matters became more desperate in Germany during 1939, there were a number of theologians and scholars in America who realized the precariousness of Bonhoeffer's situation. They invited him to Union Theological Seminary in New York City. Although Bonhoeffer had some initial doubts about coming, he finally accepted the invitation with the hope that it might provide more contacts and international resources for the cause against the Nazis. But almost immediately upon arriving in the United States, he considered the trip a mistake and decided he had to return to Germany. He wrote a letter to the American theologian and ethicist Reinhold Niebuhr, explaining:

> I must live through this difficult period of our national history with the Christian people of Germany. I will have no right to participate in the reconstruction of Christian life in Germany after the war if I do not share the trials of this time with my people. My brethren in the Confessing Synod wanted me to go. They may have been right in urging me to do so; but I was wrong in going. Such a decision each man must make for himself. Christians in Germany will face the terrible alternative of either willing the defeat of their nation in order that Christian civilization may survive, or willing the victory of their nation and thereby destroying our civilization. I know which of these alternatives I must choose; but I cannot make that choice in security. (pp. 479-80)

Bonhoeffer's action reveals the meaning of finding the true cross: just as God through Christ does not remain aloof from the terrors of human life, so we who take up the cross and follow Christ will not remain aloof from those terrors.

Bonhoeffer had arrived in the United States in June of 1939, but by July, 1939, he was back in Berlin, where he was made a civilian agent of the *Abwehr*, the German military intelligence. What his employers did not know at the time was that Bonhoeffer and others inside their organization were plotting to overthrow the government.

But after the discovery of his name on documents connected with the secret transportation of Jews to Switzerland, Bonhoeffer fell under official suspicion. From then on officials began to trace his participation in plans to kill Hitler and bring down the Third Reich. The picture book of his life contains a photograph of the prison cell, six feet by nine feet, where the police threw him after his arrest on April 5, 1943. The blankets smelled so bad from vomit and excrement that he could not cover himself with them, and he was chilled through the night.

Eventually the guard figured out that this was Dietrich Bonhoeffer of the famous Bonhoeffer family, and sometimes as a result Dietrich received preferential treatment, which he hated. But whenever this happened, he used the occasion to plead on behalf of the poorest prisoners who had no way of appealing for decent treatment. Out of this experience Bonhoeffer writes about learning "to see the great events of world history from below, from the perspective of the outcast, the suspects, the maltreated, the powerless, the oppressed, the reviled—in short, from the perspective of those who suffer." [29]

These are words of one who has found the true cross. For it is on the cross that God, creator and sustainer of all that is, comes to see "the great events of world history from below." When we find and bear the true cross as Bonhoeffer did, we come to see life "from the perspective of the outcast."

Bonhoeffer's new perspective never became the occasion for religious arrogance: he did not look down upon others less enlightened than himself. Those who find the true cross are not haughty and strident about their discovery. They do not go around bragging how they have found it. In a candid letter to his fellow conspirators which Bonhoeffer wrote at Christmas, 1942, three months before his arrest, he formulates a principle which he had learned from his own life:

> We must allow for the fact that most people learn wisdom only by personal experience. This explains, first, why so few people are capable of taking precautions in advance—they always fancy that they will somehow or other avoid the danger, till it is too late. Secondly, it explains their insensibility to the sufferings of others; sympathy grows in proportion to the fear of approaching disaster. [30]

And yet his realism about human nature does not lead Bonhoeffer to despair. In the same letter he writes about the importance of maintaining a healthy optimism, which he defines with his characteristic precision:

> The essence of optimism is not its view of the present, but the fact that it is the inspiration of life and hope when others give in. . . . There are people who regard it as frivolous, and some Christians think it impious for anyone to hope and prepare for a better earthly future. They think that the meaning of present events is chaos, disorder, and catastrophe; and in resignation or pious escapism they surrender all responsibility for reconstruction and for future generations. It may be that the day of judgment will dawn tomorrow; in that case, we shall gladly stop working for a better future. But not before. [31]

Visionary preachers are realists: realistic about the world and realistic about hope. Realism that is limited to one or the other is not realism because it does not take in the fullness of reality.

Bonhoeffer lived out his affirmation of hope and optimism in his personal as well as public life. He fell in love with Maria von Wedemeyer. Less than three months before his arrest they became engaged. Maria was sometimes able to visit Dietrich in prison, but their primary means of communication was by letter. One day he wrote to her interpreting the meaning of their relationship in the midst of so much terror and suffering:

> When [the biblical prophet] Jeremiah said, in his people's hour of direst need, that "houses and fields [and vineyards] shall again be bought in this land," it was a token of confidence in the future. That requires faith, and may God grant it to us daily. I don't mean the faith that flees the world, but the faith that endures *in* the world and loves and remains true to that world in spite of all the hardships it brings us. Our marriage must be a "yes" to God's earth. It must strengthen our resolve to do and accomplish something on earth. I fear that Christians who venture to stand on earth on only one leg will stand in heaven on only one leg too.[32]

They who find the true cross say "Yes" to God's earth. Having seen through Jesus Christ how desperately God cares for this world, they throw themselves with abandon into the struggle to bring about the world that God intends. This is how visionary preachers live, this is the gospel they proclaim to the church under reconstruction.

Near the end of the picture book of Bonhoeffer's life there is a photograph of where he was hanged. Before I read the copy that accompanies the picture I thumb back through the earlier pages. I see the pictures of the little boy with Sabine, the adolescent, the young seminary student, the seminary professor, the pastor. I turn back and forth between these pictures and the place where Bonhoeffer was hanged. I try to figure out what gave him the courage to persevere so courageously. Another human being's soul is a far country to travel to, and there are territories in every human heart that no one knows but God, even after we read someone's most profound and intimate writings. However, there is a poem that Bonhoeffer wrote in prison which brought me at least some glimpse into the far country of his soul. In the struggle and final resolution of that poem, I believe Bonhoeffer gives us a witness to how we can be as faithful and as brave as he was. The poem is titled "Who Am I?"[33] and it begins like this:

> Who am I? They often tell me
> I would step from my cell's confinement
> calmly, cheerfully, firmly,
> like a squire from his country-house.

As the poem continues, Bonhoeffer keeps repeating the question "Who am I?" and he recounts all the flattery he gets from guards and everybody else about how courageous he is. He wonders:

> Am I then really all that which other men tell of?
> Or am I only what I know of myself,
> restless and longing and sick, like a bird in a cage,
> struggling for breath, as though hands were compressing my throat,
> yearning for colours, for flowers, for the voices of birds. . .

Then, by the grace of God, comes a revelation in a final couplet, and it is a revelation of the central religious truth that marks all his writing and preaching and acting:

> Who am I? They mock me, these lonely questions of mine.
> Whoever I am, thou knowest, O God, I am thine.

This is the revelation that comes to one who has found the true cross. This is the revelation that allows one to say with redemptive trust: "Mother/Father, into your hands I commend my Spirit."

At dawn, April 9, 1945, in the execution shed of Flossenburg concentration camp, Bonhoeffer was led out to be hanged. A doctor who was present and who knew Bonhoeffer's name but nothing else about him wrote:

> Through the half-open door in one room of the huts I saw Pastor Bonhoeffer, before taking off his prison garb, kneeling on the floor praying fervently to his God. I was most deeply moved by the way this lovable man prayed, so devout and so certain that God heard his prayer. At the place of execution, he again said a short prayer and then climbed the steps to the gallows, brave and composed. His death ensued after a few seconds. In the almost fifty years that I worked as a doctor, I have hardly ever seen a man die so entirely submissive to the will of God.[34]

The last written words we have of Bonhoeffer's are to Bishop Bell, a bishop in England with whom Bonhoeffer had worked earlier in an attempt to gather ecumenical resistance to Hitler. Bonhoeffer wrote Bell: "This is the end, for me the beginning of life."[35]

At these words there is a great silence in the church under reconstruction. Neither the cloud above nor the congregation below the God-shaped hole make a sound. It is the holy silence that falls upon heaven and earth in the presence of one who has found the true cross and borne it faithfully. It is the silence that burns away all our jabberings. It is the silence that feeds the prayers too deep for words, the sighs of the Spirit sighing in our hearts. It is the silence that reminds us how costly visionary preaching can be. It is the silence that is broken by the cloud before it is broken by earth because this silence reveals how partial and incomplete all mortal knowledge is.

THE FORCES FOR GOOD SURROUND US IN WONDER

Helena is the first to speak. She tells Rufinus that she does not want to finish her legend, that Bonhoeffer's living the true search for the cross makes her more aware than ever of things that now pain her about the ancient story. But the whole cloud insists that she needs to have Rufinus finish the story. They argue that those who gather beneath the God-shaped hole will not be helped in the work of reconstructing the church if they have an idealized version of Christian traditions. A romanticized past will breed a romanticized faith in the present. Those who are blind to the inadequacies and distortions of their ancestors will be blind to the inadequacies and distortions in themselves: "While the church must sometimes preach against a text, doctrine, or practice, such elements should be kept in the memory of the Christian community to help the church continually remember its finitude."[36]

Helena at last agrees and motions to Rufinus, and he finishes recounting the legend of the true cross:

> When the queen [Helena] saw that her wish had been answered by such a clear sign [the healing of the woman who touched the true cross], she built a marvellous church of royal magnificence over the place where she had discovered the Cross. The nails, too, which had attached the Lord's body to the Cross, she sent to her son. From some of these he had a horse's bridle made, for use in battle, while he used the other to add strength to a helmet, equally with a view to using it in battle. Part of the redeeming wood she sent to her son, but she also left part of it there preserved in silver chests. This part is commemorated by regular veneration to this very day. The venerable queen also left this further proof of her deep piety: she invited to dinner the virgins whom she found there consecrated to God. She is said to have

looked after them with such great devotion, that she considered it a disgrace if they used the services of maidservants. Instead, having herself donned the garb of a maidservant, she served them food and drink with her own hands and poured water over their hands. She who was both queen of all the known world and the mother of the emperor appointed herself the servant of the servants of Christ. This, then, is the true story of what happened in Jerusalem.

While many in the cloud point out how Helena lived the meaning of the true cross through her service to others, she does not welcome their praise. She is too upset about the way the cross and the nails were used to make a horse's bridle and a helmet for battle. She had discovered the true cross, the cross of healing and restoration, and then her son, Emperor Constantine, turned it back into the cross of violence. After all her work, after her pilgrimage to Jerusalem, after finding the true cross, after building a marvelous church on the site, after all of these genuine acts of piety, her discovery still resulted in a distortion of the symbol: *O, will it ever end, this constant finding and losing the true cross?*

The question sounds simultaneously in heaven and earth and fills the God-shaped hole, its echoes haunting the vast gap between the cloud and the church under reconstruction:

O, will it ever end, end, end,
this finding, finding, finding,
and losing, losing, losing
the true cross, cross, cross . . .

For a moment profound silence falls again in heaven and earth. But then a single voice in the cloud starts to sing the last two stanzas of a hymn

Bonhoeffer wrote in December 1944, the last Christmas of his mortal life.[37]

> When now the silence deepens for our hearkening,

The entire cloud quickly joins in:

> grant we may hear thy children's voices raise
> from all the unseen world around us darkening
> their universal paean, in thy praise.

At these words of hope, the people worshiping in the church under reconstruction remember that the early church celebrated the passion, death, and resurrection of Christ as one continuously unfolding grace-filled action. The search for the true cross points beyond Calvary to the risen Christ.

By the last stanza of Bonhoeffer's hymn all those who gather beneath the God-shaped hole join in the singing. And while they praise God, the wind sweeps down and pours upon them the wisdom to see the distortions of their own faith, the strength to continue searching for the true cross, and the fire they need to be visionary preachers while the church is under reconstruction:

> While all the powers of good aid and attend us,
> boldly we'll face the future, come what may.
> At even and at morn God will befriend us,
> and oh, most surely on each newborn day!

Chapter 3

The Spirit Sighs:
Follow the Living Christ

ASLEEP OR AWAKE TO RESURRECTION

A sculptor, carrying chisel and mallet, appears in the cloud of witnesses and points to a stone carving that adorns the central panel of a fourth-century Christian sarcophagus.[1] An empty cross divides the panel vertically and horizontally. Above the crossbeam is a great wreath, the sign of victory in Roman culture. Like spokes in a wheel, the first two letters of Christ's name, *XR,* are super-imposed upon one another and fill the wreath. A dove is perched on each end of the cross beam. Arching over the whole cross is the dome of heaven.

But what grips my attention most are the two fig-ures underneath the crossbeam. On the right side there is a Roman soldier. He is sitting on a rock and propping himself up with a large battle sword. The tip is in the ground, and he has placed his arms on the hilt of the sword to form a pillow for his head. He is sound asleep.

On the opposite side of the cross is another figure, who like the soldier is sitting on a rock. It is difficult to tell if this is a man or a woman. But the other details are clear. The right hand, which is the only one we can see, is open with the palm facing upward. The head too is tilted up, and the eyes are open. All of these details are characteristic of the posture of early Christians at prayer. This praying figure looks at the *XR* circled by the wreath of victory that sits atop the cross. This praying figure, unlike the sleeping Roman soldier, sees the glory of the resurrection.

Through this sermon in stone, I hear the sculptor calling from the cloud of witnesses: "Are you asleep or awake to the resurrection? Are you praying, are you open to wonder, are you ready to receive the new life God brings out of death?"

The Wind moves through the God-shaped hole and redirects my gaze from the praying figure back to the soldier who is asleep on the sword. The Spirit is warning me not to turn too quickly to pious thoughts about the necessity of prayer until I have considered what revelation the soldier has to offer.

That soldier asleep on his sword is an evocative symbol. The sword belongs not just to the soldier but to the Roman Empire. It stands for the power of the world: brutal, domineering, certain of its position and truth. Because the soldier is completely dependent upon the world's power, he misses what is most important at the center of existence: the risen Christ, the new life that God brings forth from death.

As I train my eye on the soldier, the Wind blows again, and on the Wind comes the voice of the sculptor asking me: "O preacher, what sword are you leaning on that keeps you asleep to the resurrection?"

At first I protest. After all, I am a minister of the gospel, not a soldier, enforcing the world's values. I am not asleep to the resurrection. Quite the opposite: I am ready to preach a sermon on the sculptor's image. It will be titled "Asleep or Awake?" It will be a prophetic sermon against the militarism and violence of the world. I will attack how we rely too much on our own strength. We need to become like the figure at prayer.

But the more I outline the sermon, the more the wind howls against my words. The Spirit dismisses my sermon as homiletical cliché. It is not visionary preaching that claims the meaning of the sculptor's witness for today. The Spirit insists that before we preachers attack soldiers asleep on their swords (or guns or missiles or bombs), before we judge the spiritual somnolence of the world, we must come to terms with the dependencies and illusions that keep us oblivious to resurrection now, to the new life that God is bringing out of death. We must deal with the violence that starts in the household of God, that acknowledges how "the truth of Jesus Christ has been claimed as the sponsor of both fantastic and horrible things."[2] The wind persists in asking: "O preacher, what sword are you leaning on that keeps you asleep to the resurrection?"

RESURRECTION HERE AND NOW

Meditating upon the image, I realize that the sculptor has eschewed a literal depiction of resurrection. There is no rock rolled aside, no body tramping out of the tomb, nothing to suggest that resurrection is artificial respiration and cardiopulmonary resuscitation. Instead, the artist depends entirely on symbol: the victory wreath surrounding the XR, the birds on the cross, the posture of prayer.

Resurrection is something greater than returning to the life that once was. Jesus does not come back to carry on his ministry exactly as he did before Good Friday and Easter. Resurrection is new creation, new being. Resurrection is life in a transfigured mode. We encounter this new reality when the preacher is open to the breathwindspirit of God: "Through speech empowered by the Spirit, Jesus Christ himself is present within human consciousness."[3]

A literal picture would reveal that the sculptor is as dependent upon a constricted imagination as the soldier is on his sword. To depict the resurrection merely as the body walking out of the tomb would offer little comfort to the family and friends feeling the undeniable void of their loss. The artist cares for the mourners through a vision that reminds them the risen Christ is not buried in static images of the first Easter. The risen Christ comes here and now to those who pray.

While I reflect on the wisdom of the artist's sermon, the Spirit identifies what keeps us preachers as soundly asleep to the resurrection as the soldier's sword. Our sword is the Bible. Our sword is religious cliché. Our sword is Jesusolatry: confining Christ to images of the itinerant preacher walking the hills of Palestine. Our sword is talking about the resurrection as past event or future hope but never present reality. Our sword is theological rigidity that blocks us from being open to resurrection here and now:

> What we hanker after is a sign from heaven which cannot be spoken against, an experience in which we are lifted out of the tears and sweat and dirt of our humanity into a serene empyrean where the gritty quality of our ordinary daily life is left far behind and can be forgotten. But resurrection as a present miracle does not deliver us from the unevenness and turmoil and fragmentariness of being human. The miracle is to be found precisely within the ordinary round and daily

routine of our lives. Resurrection occurs to us as we are, and its coming is generally quiet and unobtrusive and we may hardly be aware of its creative power. It is often only later that we realize that in some way or other we have been raised to newness of life, and so have heard the voice of the Eternal Word.[4]

Our propensity to "hanker" after being lifted "into a serene empyrean" takes many forms, but perhaps the most common is what I call "biblicism." I use this word to indicate a religiosity that confuses a relationship to the living Christ with an obsession with scriptural texts. Biblicist versions of Christianity forget that God does not call us to return to the letter of the law but to follow Christ, and "we are summoned to preach the gospel not the Bible."[5] Furthermore, the gospel is not simply one of the four books written by the biblical evangelists: "the gospel is the good news of God's redemptive presence and purposes in the world."[6] Gospel is the gracious impulse of God that sets all authentic witnesses to God into motion: "The Gospel was there before the Bible, and it created the Bible, as it creates the true preacher and the true sermon everywhere."[7]

There is fundamentalist biblicism which claims to take the Scriptures literally, and there is scholarly biblicism that gets so entangled in exegetical detail that it never risks making bold theological interpretations. In either case, debates about the meaning of the text become all consuming, and the disputants fail to ask the urgent questions of a post-Easter faith:

Where is the risen Christ now?

Where is resurrection happening in this life?

How will we respond?

At these questions a great chorus of witnesses gathers in the God-shaped hole. The sculptor, using

FOLLOW THE LIVING CHRIST

his chisel as a baton, conducts the cloud in a cele-
bration of resurrection here and now.

> Christ is alive! Let Christians sing.
> His cross stands empty to the sky.
> Let streets and homes with praises ring.
> Love, drowned in death, shall never die.

> Christ is alive! No longer bound
> to distant years in Palestine,
> but saving, healing, here and now,
> and touching every place and time.

> In every insult, rift and war,
> where colour, scorn or wealth divide,
> Christ suffers still, yet loves the more,
> and lives, where even hope has died.

> Women and men, in age and youth,
> can feel the Spirit, hear the call,
> and find the way, the life, the truth,
> revealed in Jesus, freed for all.

> Christ is alive, and comes to bring
> good news to this and every age,
> till earth and sky and ocean ring
> with joy, with justice, love and praise.[8]

When the sculptor and chorus have finished, I call out
to them that I am baffled by their performance. They
have just sung a hymn by a living hymn writer. I am
surprised to discover they are learning new music
with all the riches they have brought with them from
the centuries. The cloud lets out a sigh of exaspera-
tion that echoes against the walls of the church under
reconstruction. The sculptor explains that heaven is
continually renewed by bursts of the wind coming
from every direction, including the gusts that blow
through those who give fresh expression to the
gospel:

> Christ is alive! No longer bound
> to distant years in Palestine,
> but saving, healing, here and now,
> and touching every place and time.

The poetry recapitulates what the sculptor expressed in stone: Christ is alive. Resurrection happens here and now and is accessible to those who have the grace to pray, to open themselves to the reality through a posture of prayer and trust.

THE PRESENT-TENSE CHRIST

When the sculptor created the image on the sarcophagus around 350 C.E., the biblical canons (there is more than one) had not yet taken their final shape. But that did not stop the risen Christ from inspiring the artist. It did not hold Christ back from comforting the mourners who opened themselves to the divine presence through prayer and trust. Christ was no less alive when there was no Bible than Christ was after the Bible was gathered together. The Bible did not raise Christ to new life. God did.

The Bible often displaces God in popular piety. As Pastor Valerie Brown Troutman, whose ministry shows a deep respect for the Scriptures, observes: "People have been taught that the Bible is God. But the Bible is not God. But someone has done a good job convincing them the Bible is God."[9]

Visionary preachers do not use the Bible like the soldier's sword. They do not lean so hard on the Bible that they fall asleep to the risen Christ coming to them here and now. They do not fall into one of the most common traps of so-called "biblical" preaching:

> Frequently biblical preaching has told a biblical story replete with oodles of biblical background, a "holy history," but has not permitted God to step out of the biblical world into human history. The God of biblical preaching has been a past-tense God of past-tense events whose past-tense truth ("original meaning") may be *applied* to the world, while God remains hidden within a gilt-edged book.[10]

The risen Christ is not a "past-tense" Christ but a present-tense Christ, one who lives among us here and now, comforts us here and now, calls us here and now, challenges us here and now.

To follow the living Christ does not mean we will abandon the Bible. In fact, it has exactly the opposite effect. Following the living Christ frees us to use the Bible with more integrity:

> To be biblical may well mean to move beyond the Bible itself to the larger principles that can be derived from the Christian faith of which the Bible is a part, but for which the Bible cannot possibly be a substitute . . . this invariably means giving more attention to the Bible and more rather than less care to its study and interpretation.[11]

Instead of trying to reconcile hopelessly conflicted passages of scripture with one another or whacking verses out of shape to make them address perspectives and issues the ancient writers never foresaw, we are liberated to appreciate the wisdom and the foolishness of the Scriptures. We can see *as an act of faithfulness to the living Christ* that the biblical writers were as inspired and as limited by their time and place as we are by ours. And we as visionary preachers can acknowledge to God, to ourselves, and to our congregations that there is great tension between the past and the present.

Visionary preachers do not deny the tension between inherited belief and contemporary experience. They cultivate the tension as a way of opening themselves to the living Christ. The witnesses in the cloud recount that it was the tension between their ancestors' belief and their own lived experience that again and again revitalized the church's theology and inspired its most meaningful expression. A living scholar summarizes what the poets in the cloud affirm: "the reconciliation of inherited theological belief with personal experience is what provides the poetic tension in an extraordinary variety of works that include the book of Job, *Paradise Lost*, and Dante's *Divine Comedy*."[12]

This tension, dramatically apparent in the work of the poets, is common to visionary preachers: although their experience is shaped by their theological inheritance, the two never fit perfectly together. The tension that results may often be uncomfortable but it is also a blessing. For it is rooted in something greater than the preacher's psyche. It is rooted in Christ, who is not confined to the Bible and the past. The risen Christ has not stopped growing and changing with history. We have a technical term for people who do not change: dead. If Christ has not changed since the resurrection, then Christ is no longer alive. But I know Christ is alive. I keep meeting Christ through people and events and prayer and at the altar when I take the bread and wine and feed on Christ in my heart by faith with thanksgiving.

A biblicist may fire at me the familiar verse, "Jesus Christ is the same yesterday and today and forever" (Hebrews 13:8). But the Gospels depict Jesus changing through his childhood days onward. If Jesus has stopped changing, he is no longer the Jesus of yesterday. I recall the Bible verse (Luke 2:52) I memorized as a child in Sunday school that was offered as a model for our growing up. I do not have to look it up because I can still hear the voice of my Sunday school teacher teaching us the words: "And Jesus *increased* in wisdom and stature and in favor with God and man." (This was in the days before inclusive language.)

The process did not stop once Jesus was an adult. The Gospels picture him developing a more inclusive vision of his ministry. The Canaanite woman who pleads with Jesus to heal her daughter compels him to expand the scope of his mission (Matthew 15:21-28; compare Mark 7:24-30). Since Jesus amplifies the understanding of his mission during his initial ministry, there is no reason to believe that the risen Christ is any less able to become more embracing of the entire human family. An unchanging Christ is not the Christ of yesterday but a different Christ from the one presented in the Bible.

The church abuses the living Christ every time it denigrates the value of any human group on the basis of a constricted biblicism. This is what led to scriptural justifications of slavery, the denial of full equality to women, and the condemnation of scientific worldviews at variance with ancient cosmologies. Nowadays biblicism is feeding the evil of rejecting gays and lesbians for full membership in the church. Those who refuse to recognize that God creates a multiplicity of sexualities lure their opponents into debating the interpretation of a few isolated scriptural passages. The exegeses grow exponentially, each side acting as if its interpretation of the Scriptures will finally settle the problem. This is biblicism at its worst: using hermeneutical warfare to circumvent the living Christ, who through the ages has shown an ever growing capacity to embrace more and more of the human family.

Visionary preachers take a different approach to such conflicts. Eschewing biblicism, they affirm

> that *the Word of God is not identical with the biblical texts.* The story of these texts is experienced as God's Word when it is heard in communities of faith and struggle as a witness to God's love for the world. This hearing is a gift of the Holy Spirit, which empowers the words so that they may transform lives. In this process of new hearing, the scriptural and church traditions are constantly in need of critique and new interpretation if they are to be liberated as a witness to new situations, cultural perspectives, and challenges.[13]

• Visionary preachers meet the living Christ through their participation in this process of new

101

hearing, new seeing, new receiving, and new creating.

- Visionary preachers trust that Jesus Christ is today the same dynamic, changing Jesus Christ as he was yesterday and forever.
- Visionary preachers know that they can be wrong in understanding how Jesus Christ is changing, so they test their visions with the church that gathers beneath the God-shaped hole. They realize that Christ moves not just in the individual heart but among the community of faith.
- Visionary preachers seek to be faithful by living with the tension that is in Christ's own being: the tension between the faith of the past and the new demands of the present.

NO LONGER IN COMMAND

Tension is not something most of us welcome. Tension means that we are no longer in command, that life and death, faith and God are not ours to control. All of us sometimes and some of us all the time are like the soldier asleep on his sword: we prefer to rest on the world's securities or if not the world's, then the church's. We cling to a form of belief that ensures God will not pull any surprises. We are like the religious authorities in Matthew: we do not want resurrection. Although their ostensible reason for going to Pilate is to warn him that Jesus' followers may dig up the body, their jitters suggest a deeper motivation:

> Beneath the fear that they spoke about to Pilate lay another fear that they had not spoken about to anyone probably, not even to each other. This was the fear which I doubt very much if any one of them had had the courage to face more than fleetingly even within

the secrecy of his own heart—the fear that the man whom they had crucified would *really* come alive again as he had promised, that the body that now lay dead in its tomb, disfigured by the mutilations of the Cross, that this body or some new and terrible version of it would start to breathe again, stand up in its grave clothes and move toward them with unspeakable power.[14]

If there were a resurrection, then the religious authorities would have less control over Christ than they did while he roamed the Galilean countryside and paraded through the streets of Jerusalem! But before we judge the authorities, let us judge ourselves. Let us judge all the ways that we try to keep resurrection from happening so that we can stay in control of Jesus and use his name to command others: arguing endlessly about doctrine and scriptural interpretation while we fail to care for Christ among the least of our sisters and brothers, refusing the new gifts that the risen Christ offers for our worship and praise, constricting our imaginings of Christ to images that leave us comfortable and undisturbed. All of these fall under the general category of Jesusolatry: avoiding the living Christ by freezing Jesus in the past.

The renowned cinematographer Ingmar Bergman provides a striking witness to how Jesusolatry can shut out faith from a heart that is otherwise open to the living Christ. Bergman writes, "I have also said good-bye to the film about Jesus. Too long, too many togas, too many quotations."[15] What turns Bergman off is an imagining of Jesus that is too mired in biblicism and its accompanying Jesusolatry. But Bergman is not closed to the living Christ. He is open to what H. A. Williams described above as "the miracle" that "is to be found precisely within the ordinary round and daily routine of our lives." Bergman realizes that "if you peel off the layers of various theologies, the holy always remains," and this realization empowers him to write:

> Christ, most beloved. Suffering is not difficult if you know your mission. True suffering comes from knowing the commandment of love and seeing how human beings betray themselves and each other when it comes to love. How they defile love. Christ's clearsightedness must have caused his greatest suffering.[16]

Peeling off theological layers to reveal the holy is what the resurrection does. The busted tomb is like the God-shaped hole in the roof:

> We have everything fixed in place in our minds.
> Our world is neatly ordered.
> Solid.
> Bounded.
> Indisputable.
> We know what life is.
> We know what death is.
> Oh, we are so wise.
> Our belief so secure.
> Our faith so well defined.
> Then: resurrection!
> God destroys our certainty.
> Terror and amazement seize us.
> We have lost control.
> Lost control of the world we knew.
> Worse yet:
> lost control of God,
> lost control of Christ.

Since death, the one absolutely inviolable limit to life, is no longer fixed in place, it follows that we cannot rely on any other absolutism, including human articulations of religious belief. Resurrection marks the end of theological triumphalism. The relativism of visionary preaching is born of a passionate faith in the risen Christ. For the resurrection has revealed the transitory nature of all that we assume to be fixed. Religious rigidities are as effective in trapping Christ as the stone at the tomb. Resurrection shatters them all and leaves a God-shaped hole revealing the never-to-be-controlled realities of Christ, the wind, and the cloud of witnesses.

THE TERROR OF RESURRECTION

Resurrection is the last thing in the world that the religiously rigid want to acknowledge. They run to post a guard of soldiers every time Christ threatens to break from the tomb: the living Christ who refuses to limit his actions to the patterns of ministry recorded two thousand years ago, the living Christ who challenges us to believe the full implication of the astounding claim that he is not buried in Palestine. If the authorities could not silence and control Jesus in Palestine, why do we think we can control the risen Christ?

The resurrection of Christ is terrifying before it is empowering. Mark knows that. He ends his Gospel with the women fleeing the tomb in "terror and amazement" and saying "nothing to anyone" (Mark 16:8). Mark has the courage to face up to what resurrection means: the followers have no more control over Christ than those who refuse to acknowledge Christ.

Resurrection gives more freedom to Christ than most believers want their savior to have. Later editors cooked up their own ending to Mark's Gospel in an attempt to tame the terror of Christ's freedom.

The ancient fear of the risen Christ returns again and again. It is what drives people to patch up the God-shaped hole in the roof of the church with simplistic theological solutions: old-time religion, return to the Bible, preaching that aims to make scriptural texts come alive. The point of the gospel is not to make the Bible live now, but to present the living Christ to living people here and now. Christ does not say "Follow the Bible" but "Follow me." The twentieth-century poet Zbigniew Herbert helps us understand why this is frightening. Herbert's deceptively simple poem is titled "Meditations of Mr. Cogito on Redemption." The title is significant. Mr. Cogito's name is taken from the writings of the French philosopher René Descartes (1596–1650). Descartes made one of the most quoted statements in the history of western philosophy, *cogito ergo sum*, "I think, therefore I am." This assertion and all the reflection that attended upon it had a profound impact upon European thought and religion. It helped to lift reason to the highest place of honor. When we read "Meditations of Mr. Cogito on Redemption" we are reading the thoughts of someone who rests upon the power of reason as completely as the Roman soldier carved on the sarcophagus rests upon his sword. Mr. Cogito says of God:

He should not have sent his son

too many have seen
his son's pierced hands
his ordinary skin

it was written
to reconcile us
by the worst reconciliation

too many nostrils
have breathed with delight
the odour of his fear

one should not descend
low
fraternize with blood

he should not have sent his son
it was better to reign
in a baroque palace made out of marble clouds
on a throne of terror
with a sceptre of death.[17]

Although the poem is about more than resurrection, the closing lines reveal the human terror of losing control. Mr. Cogito wants a god who will keep life ordered by enforcing the accepted limits of reality, a deity who rules with "the sceptre of death," not one who overcomes death through resurrection. Mr. Cogito implies that if God will act reasonably, then there will be a clear hierarchy of power starting in "a baroque palace made out of marble clouds." Mr. Cogito's god would give divine justification to all the reasonable hierarchies of power on earth: the military hierarchies that have reasoned us into the possibility of nuclear destruction, the economic growth hierarchies that have reasoned us to the possibility of environmental extinction, the religious hierarchies that have reasoned us into theological positions that threaten the church with death by spiritual stagnation.

But God does not reason as Mr. Cogito does. By raising Christ, God crumbles our obsession with keeping control. Our obsession, however, is so great that it keeps returning again and again. We do not want resurrection, we want control. We want to be like the Roman soldier securely resting on his sword. We want to be in command. The peculiar form this obsession takes in our age is technology.

SALVATION 5.1: THE THEOLOGICAL DELUSIONS OF TECHNOLOGY

A few years ago, one of my homiletics students, who had preached an incoherent sermon, was

107

bewildered that no one could follow what he had said. He informed me that he had written his manuscript on the newest computer program, as if that would guarantee a comprehensible sermon! Listening to him was like listening to Mr. Cogito in person. The student's tone of voice and demeanor suggested: how could the sermon be incoherent? Everything he used to write the sermon was "state of the art." From the way the student spoke, I might have thought the software was "Salvation 5.1."

The student was giving expression to a worldview that pervades our culture: a delusive religious belief in the saving power of technology that is assumed even by secularist scientists and engineers. They view the meaning of their work through mythic constructions inherited from Mr. Cogito's distorted form of Christianity.

David F. Noble traces how Christian theology has fed our misplaced hopes for salvation through control.[18] Visionary preachers need to know this history so that they are not sucked into the delusion themselves. Resting on technology as the Roman soldier rests on his sword, we may be asleep to the resurrection.

As I recount David Noble's story of the marriage between Christian theology and technology, each historic figure he discusses appears in the cloud and calls through the God-shaped hole:

Learn from us.
Do not overestimate the value of what you create.
Give up the theological delusions of salvation by technology.
Stay awake to resurrection.

The figures gather in a growing chorus that repeats the warning from the cloud again and again. The members of the chorus see across the ages what they could not see when they were mired in the limitations of their immediate historic existence. Their new perspective saddens them for the arrogance they once displayed, and it puts a note of alarm in their voices as they call to us:

Learn from us.
Do not overestimate the value of what you create.
Give up the theological delusions of salvation
by technology.
Stay awake to resurrection.

David Noble begins his history with St. Augustine, who considered the practical arts, what we now call "technology," to be only a fragmentary enhancement of our fallen state. John Scotus Erigena, a ninth-century Benedictine, reversed this perspective and saw them as a means of reclaiming the image of God in humanity. The "mechanical arts," as he called them, were not antithetical to salvation but a means toward it.

Erigena's perspective coalesced with a renewed millenarianism in the twelfth century, especially through the writing of Joachim of Fiore, who developed a systematic interpretation of the Apocalypse of St. John which featured the important role of new technologies in ushering in the reign of God. This interpretation subsequently had a great impact upon Roger Bacon, who urged the Pope to develop the useful arts because he was convinced that the Antichrist would employ them for evil purposes, and these perils "would be easy to meet, if prelates and princes promoted study and investigated the secrets of nature and art" (p. 27).

The result of the marriage between a positive theological appreciation of the useful arts and millenarianism was that "Technology now became at the same time eschatology" (p. 22). And since heaven's reign on earth could not begin until a pre-ordained number of people were saved, global exploration became an evangelical necessity, which in turn contributed to the growing knowledge of geography and nautical science.

After the explorations of Columbus, the "New World" fed dreams of finding utopia as an actual place. Although there were various utopian visions, all of them shared a high valuation of the useful arts. In utopia everyone would be skilled in practicing technology. This was not merely to make for a satisfying material existence. It was to help restore humanity to the prelapsarian state of Adam, who during the seventeenth century, especially in England, became the subject of extensive exegetical and theological commentary. Unlike in Augustine's writings, Adam was now held to be a master of the useful arts. Therefore, the restoration of paradise required that people become, as was Adam, technologically proficient. It sounds not unlike our visions of every student becoming computer literate.

> Learn from us.
> Do not overestimate the value of what you create.
> Give up the theological delusions of salvation by technology.
> Stay awake to resurrection.

The theologically blessed expansion of technical mastery over the material world suffused the thought of scientists, philosophers, and poets so that no less a figure than John Milton could write that nature "would surrender to man as its appointed governor, and his rule would extend from command of the earth and seas to dominion over the stars" (p. 48).

Inventors and scientists began to believe that the most accurate knowledge of any phenomenon involved understanding how it was made. This was something greater than Adamic knowledge, it was divine knowledge, an understanding of the Creator's perspective. The expanded domain of cognition meant that scientists "began to assume the mantle of creator in their own right, as gods themselves" (p. 67).

Learn from us.
Do not overestimate the value of what you create.
Give up the theological delusions of salvation by
    technology.
Stay awake to resurrection.

Even as science and those who wrote about it began to divorce themselves from their theological roots, they continued to maintain in a new guise the millenarian and perfectionist visions. Thus, Robert Owen, who considered all religious belief erroneous, still saw the potential for human deliverance through advances in technology, and his followers were convinced the steam engine would be one of the gods in the state of bliss.

The historical process that began in medieval Europe culminates in America, where "as nowhere else before or since, the useful arts became wedded to Adamic myths and millenarian dreams" (p. 88). Walt Whitman supplies words that sustain Noble's claim: "I, chanter of Adamic songs, through the new garden the West." "Divine am I, inside and out, and I make holy what I touch" (p. 89). The poet's extravagant lyrics were confirmed by the famous American inventor Thomas Edison, who linked together the revelations of God and science, and Jacob Bigelow, a

Harvard professor who introduced the term "technology" to America and described its practitioners as those "who heaven's own image wear" (p. 93).

Learn from us.
Do not overestimate the value of what you create.
Give up the theological delusions of salvation by technology.
Stay awake to resurrection.

The theologically sanctioned delusion of human control through technology continues to the present moment. Mr. Cogito remains alive and well. His passion for control is manifest in our explorations of space, artificial intelligence, and genetic engineering. Faith in the living Christ does not censor exploration and experimentation. Quite the opposite: faith in the living Christ sustains intellectual curiosity. What concerns me is the illusory hope that accompanies our efforts: believing we can attain salvation through human control. To name this delusion does not make me, who uses a computer daily, or anyone else a Luddite. There are computer scientists and scholars from various disciplines who raise similar concerns. Many of them, attending an academic conference on the topic, argued that computers

> capture and enhance one kind of human thinking— based on calculation and logic—that is powerful but limited [Mr. Cogito!]. They do nothing to enhance moral intuition, imagination, emotional thinking, and a disciplined will, the critics said. The intensive use of computers with young children can actually stunt those qualities, some suggested, adding that they are all the more important if students are to be taught to manipulate powerful new technologies that can be used in constructive or destructive ways.[19]

David Noble describes how the developers of powerful new technologies often employ the language of Christian myth and theology to explain and justify their faith in what they are doing. The first "effort to put a man into space was called Adam" (p. 126). A leading pioneer in Artificial Intelligence (AI), Edward Fredkin, was convinced that AI was the only way to salvation and that through a "global algorithm" we would achieve "peace and harmony" (p. 154). Walter Gilbert, a researcher involved with the double helix molecule, saw through his work "a vision of the grail" (p. 191). And these are but a few verbal fragments from a coherently woven theological superstructure whose assumptions and values go largely unchallenged.

In many cases, the scientists are not secularists but Christians who self-consciously draw upon the traditional language of faith to interpret the meaning of their work. However, their identification with the church does not lessen the propensity to make overextended claims for technology. Instead, their faith often makes things worse because they are unwilling to offer the severe critique of tradition that women and two-thirds world theologians have been making within the church for several decades. Their faith does not recognize the God-shaped hole that characterizes the church under reconstruction. Thus Donald Munro, an evangelical Christian geneticist, comforts himself about the possible misuse of his research: "God will ensure that we don't go too far afield" (p. 196). Does the man know nothing at all about the horrors that God has allowed us to do to one another throughout history? Has he no sense of sin?

Learn from us.
Do not overestimate the value of what you create.
Give up the theological delusions of salvation by technology.
Stay awake to resurrection.

Although David Noble incisively describes how Christian beliefs have fed the delusion of salvation through technology, he tends to treat Christian theology as a single, coherent stream. But in fact there are multiple streams of Christian thought, many of them in conflict. If certain kinds of Christian theology have been as influential as Noble claims in perpetuating our illusory expectations for technology, then it will take a less distorted form of theology to correct them. It will take a theology that does not reinforce our obsession with control, a theology that is awake to resurrection, alert to the astonishing openings and novel possibilities which we have yet to encounter.

READING CHRIST IN THE HEART

Visionary preachers give up the delusion of control. They become like the praying figure opposite the Roman soldier on the sarcophagus. Having no sword, no false expectation of salvation through technology to lean upon, they remain awake to the resurrection. Visionary preachers stand in spirit with the illiterate slave whom Melva Costen describes: "Approached about the depth of her understanding of the gospel message, she replied: 'I can't read a word. But I read Jesus in my heart. . . . I knows he's there 'cause I read him in my heart, just like you know about him from reading the book!' "[20] This slave speaks to us from the cloud with a wisdom and a spiritual genius that reveal the delusions of the Mr. Cogitos and the technocrats of this world.

The slave masters deliberately kept their slaves, whom they considered chattel, illiterate. They feared reading would foster liberation. They would lose control of their slaves. But since the risen Christ is not confined to the pages of the Bible, the masters lost control anyway. The slave received the risen Christ in her heart.

Reading Christ in the heart is more than sweet pietism. It is a revolutionary statement. The efforts of the slave masters to remain in command are futile against the risen Christ. The very activity that the master wants to suppress goes on in a new way: "I can't read a word. But I read Jesus in my heart." The slave's reading is as authoritative as the reading of the master. The slave knows Jesus in her own way "just like you know him from reading the book!" The slave is the full equal of the master: able to read and knowing Christ.

The slave woman's witness to Christ in the heart reveals the delusion of human control for what it is: a delusion. We cannot control the risen Christ

by oppression
by biblicism
by technology.

All three share this in common: they are obsessed with the controlling function of language but their obsession is to no avail. The slave master is not able to keep the risen Christ from entering the slave's heart. The biblicist is not able to command how Christ will grow and change. And the technocrat is not able to program where the wind will blow. Joseph Weizenbaum, a professor emeritus of computer science at the Massachusetts Institute of Technology, has "recalled speaking with students who are unable to imagine human experiences that cannot be directly and completely expressed in words. Whatever can be captured in words, their thinking goes, can at least theoretically be programmed into a machine."[21]

The risen Christ calls us to let go of our obsession with control, an obsession that begins with our theological anxiety to plug up the God-shaped

hole with an image that will stay put, an image that
will give us the fixed order that Mr. Cogito craves.
We are invited to leave behind idolatrous certitude
for an ever deepening relationship to the living
Christ. Like the wide-awake figure on the sarcophagus, we take a posture of spiritual attentiveness
and pray:

> O Christ, my Lord, again and again
> I have said with Mary Magdalene,
> "They have taken away my Lord
> and I know not where they have laid him."
> I have been desolate and alone.
> And thou hast found me again, and I know
> that what has died is not thou, my Lord,
> but only my idea of thee,
> the image which I have made to preserve
> what I have found, and to be my security.
> I shall make another image, O Lord,
> better than the last.
> That too must go, and all successive images,
> until I come to the blessed vision of thyself,
> O Christ, my Lord.[22]

The more we live the spirit of this prayer, the
less anxious we become about preaching in the
church with the God-shaped hole. The God-shaped
hole invites us to preach not answers but the living
Christ. Resurrection is no longer simply the once-a-
year theme of Easter, but it becomes for us the pattern that H. A. Williams says it is: a "miracle [that]
is to be found precisely within the ordinary round
and daily routine of our lives."

- Resurrection is the opening of astonishing new
  possibilities when we give up the delusion that
  we control reality.
- Resurrection is the renewed love that friends,
  partners, and spouses discover when they let go
  of their need to reform the other.

- Resurrection is the vital ministry that results when a church releases its obsession with doing things as they always have.
- Resurrection is the fresh impulse that inspires artists when they acknowledge they have for too long been working one creative vein.
- Resurrection is the surprising discovery of scientists who put aside an old theory in order to examine unexpected data.
- Resurrection is the transformation of preaching that occurs when a preacher decides to risk entirely new ways of creating and delivering sermons.
- Resurrection is the future that opens to a society when it comes to terms with its injustice and prejudice.
- Resurrection is "the blessed vision of thyself, / O Christ, my Lord" that is granted when we finally release the images which we have made to preserve what we have found and to be our security.

Release and receive. Release and receive. That is the pattern of those who greet the risen Christ. They release what they have gripped so they can open themselves to new reality. Mary releases the Jesus she had known in order to live by faith in the risen Christ.

Releasing our images of Christ is not a single, once-and-for-all action, but a process of maturation that continues throughout our lives:

> I shall make another image, O Lord,
> better than the last.
> That too must go, and all successive images,
> until I come to the blessed vision of thyself,
> O Christ, my Lord.

While I pray these words for myself, I hear a single voice thundering "Amen, Amen." I look up to the cloud and see once more John Donne, the famous poet/preacher, whose cry "'Tis all in pieces, all coherence gone" sounded when I first decided to wait beneath the God-shaped hole.[23]

If anybody ever knew and expressed in magnificent language the long hard process of giving up control and finally becoming open to the risen Christ, it was John Donne. Most of his life he was anything but an exemplary Christian. He is, as one of my colleagues observed, "a particularly good case of what God has to overcome and does overcome."[24] Not a promising subject for hagiography, Donne is close to us in our foibles and passions, yet he is gifted with a genius for language that expresses the struggle to stay awake to resurrection. It was a struggle that continued for this poet/preacher into the final days of his life.

THE WHOLE COURSE OF OUR LIFE

February 25, 1631. John Donne is in bed, dying of stomach cancer. He has one last engagement to preach before the court and king, and he is working on his sermon outline. His friends urge him not to go. But the poet/preacher pulls himself out of bed, dresses, gets to the service and delivers one of his greatest sermons. He declares to the congregation: "Our *criticall* day is not the *very day* of our *death*: but the whole course of our life. I thanke him that *prayes* for me when the *Bell* tolls, but I thank him much more that *Catechises* mee, or *preaches* to mee, or *instructs mee how to live*."[25]

When Donne returned from preaching and lay down knowing the end was close, perhaps the words of his sermon echoed in his own heart. They often do in us preachers. Who had instructed Donne how to live?

Scenes from the man's life and the vision of him in the cloud of witnesses alternate in my imagination. The poet/preacher in the cloud is sometimes delighted, sometimes horrified at what he did, wrote, and preached on earth. He was often asleep to resurrection, as dependent upon the world, its values and affirmations as the soldier upon his sword. But at other times, the grace of God opened John Donne to the living Christ, who then inspired his poems and sermons.[26]

Perhaps as Donne was dying, he recalled his childhood home on Bread Street in London. He may have had the faintest memory of his father, who died when he was four years old but who often preceded the Lord Mayor of London as he moved in procession through the city.

Interwoven with these fond recollections must have been the terror of being Roman Catholic in a nation where that religious affiliation was often seen as traitorous. John Donne as a child knew profound fear, fear for the life of his relatives and later on fear for his own life. Roman Catholics had been disemboweled, drawn and quartered, sometimes merely because their belief made them suspect to the state. Although John Donne would later renounce his Roman Catholicism, his consciousness was forever stamped by that upbringing.

The terror of religious persecution left a chilling impact upon Donne's work. After having become Anglican, he decried in some of his sermons those Roman Catholics who tried to hide their continuing religious allegiance to Rome. As Donne lay dying, was he haunted by these sermons? Was he pained by the memory that after he had converted he sometimes preached the same prejudice under which he had suffered?

There is every probability that as death

approached, Donne kept working to pull together the pieces of his life. For the great theme of his life's work was the search for meaning in a fragmented world. The need to find meaning in a shattered world fueled Donne's art and sermons just as the God-shaped hole drives the work of preachers in the church under reconstruction. Donne had a "passion for fusion or interpenetration."[27] His contemporaries compared him to Copernicus, the great astronomer who had demonstrated that the earth revolves around the sun. As Copernicus revolutionized cosmology so Donne was revolutionizing literature as he struggled to bring together the new science and the inherited religious tradition which was reeling from the new discoveries about the universe. If Donne had been a biblicist, if he had retreated into a state of denial about the God-shaped hole of his own era, Donne would not have been awake to the risen Christ. It was living creatively with the tension of his age that made Donne a powerful poet and the most compelling preacher of his generation.

We can see Donne's propensity for "fusion or interpenetration" at work in his Holy Sonnet VII about the day of judgment. He opens with a precise observation about the planet earth as a globe and then goes on to consider the existential meaning of final judgment for the present life:

> At the round earths imagin'd corners, blow
> Your trumpets, Angells, and arise, arise
> From death, you numberlesse infinities
> Of soules, and to your scattred bodies goe,
> All whom the flood did, and fire shall o'erthrow,
> All whom warre, dearth, age, agues [fevers], tyrannies
> Despaire, law, chance, hath slaine, and you whose eyes,
> Shall behold God, and never tast deaths woe.
> But let them sleepe, Lord, and mee mourne a space,
> For, if above all these, my sinnes abound,
> 'Tis late to aske abundance of thy grace,
> When wee are there; here on this lowly ground,

Teach mee how to repent; for that's as good
As if thou'hadst seal'd my pardon, with thy blood.
   (p. 249)

The language may sound dated to our ears, but if we place this sonnet in the context of the scientific revolution that was sending intellectual earthquakes through the world of faith, then we can see Donne's imaginative daring. In the fourteen compressed lines of a sonnet he blends global exploration and one of the great theological themes of medieval Christianity: the judgment day.

Donne redefines the judgment day in two distinctly modern ways. First of all he acknowledges the impact of science on religion. Religious literalism is replaced by an awareness of the role of the imagination: "At the round earths *imagin'd* corners, blow / Your trumpets, Angells." And second, Donne refocuses our spiritual attention by stressing the current existential meaning of divine judgment: "*here* on this lowly ground, / Teach mee how to repent." Donne dazzles us with a vision of judgment day and then uses this apocalyptic frenzy to drive home the point of it all: that we are to remake our lives here and now in this world. This is not only splendid poetry. It is powerful preaching. It is being awake to the living Christ who inspires a witness that is profoundly true to the meaning of the scriptures for Donne's own age.

Because Donne is so courageous in making leaps between new knowledge and the meaning of ancient tradition in his poetry and preaching, it would not surprise me if his perpetually active mind continued the search for meaning even while he lay dying. Perhaps his thoughts roamed back to his years at Oxford University where he matriculated in 1584 at the age of twelve. He started at such a young age because when students turned sixteen they were required to affirm the Thirty-Nine Articles of the Church of England, an affirmation which constituted heresy for a Roman Catholic. By beginning the University at such an early age Donne could complete his education before being required to reject his faith.

We are not exactly sure when, but sometime in his teens John Donne transferred to Cambridge University. Cambridge was the more literary university at the time, and while he was there Donne sharpened his literary wit and his mastery of classical rhetoric, skills that later helped to make him the greatest English preacher of his day.

Long before Donne became a preacher, he aspired to upward social mobility in court and society. In a portrait, done about 1595, when he was in his early twenties, he poses as a melancholy lover. I look from the portrait to Donne, the great preacher in the cloud of witnesses who is blushing at his youthful excess. But then he regains his composure and calls down through the God-shaped hole that the sermons, their passion and power, are not understandable apart from all of his work, including his love poems. He warns that nobody will take seriously preachers who are in denial of their full humanity, including their sexuality. Where there is no passion, there will be no visionary preaching. We will not be awake to the risen Christ.

A twentieth-century poet, C. H. Sisson, joins in support of Donne and helps us understand that the passion of the poet fed the credibility of his witness to Christ:

> I understand you well enough, John Donne
> First, that you were a man of ability
> Eaten by lust and the love of God
> Then, that you crossed the Sevenoaks High Street
> As rector of Saint Nicholas:
> I am of that parish.
> . . . .

Come down and speak to the men of ability
On the Sevenoaks platform and tell them
That at your Saint Nicholas the faith
Is not exclusive in the fools it chooses
That the vain, the ambitious and the highly sexed
Are the natural prey of the incarnate Christ.[28]

Whether or not Donne's love poems sprang from particular relationships we cannot say with certainty. Scholars debate these matters. But one thing is clear: much of John Donne's rhapsodic excess reflects the literary conventions of his age. Readers expected exaggeration and hyperbole in poems of love. Nevertheless, in Donne's poetry these take a unique form. Unlike many other famous poets of love, Donne rarely includes any description of the beloved. Instead, his love poems are marked with an unusual degree of intellectual complexity. Donne lavishes his poetic splendors not on the beloved herself but on the significance and effect of their love. For example, here is the poet berating the morning sun for interrupting a night of love:

Busie old foole, unruly Sunne,
Why dost thou thus,
Through windowes and through curtaines call on us?
Must to thy motions lovers seasons run?
Sawcy, pedantique wretch, goe chide
Late schoole boys, and sowre prentices,
Goe tell Court-huntsmen, that the King will ride,
Call countrey ants to harvest offices;
Love, all alike, no season knowes, nor clyme,
Nor houres, dayes, moneths, which are the rags of time.
. . . .
                    and since thy duties bee
     To warme the world, that's done in warming us.
Shine here to us, and thou art every where;
This bed thy center is, these walls, thy sphaere. (p. 11)

The world that is in pieces finds a new center, a new source of meaning in the love shared by poet and

123

beloved. What seems nothing more than a romantic conceit, our love is the center of the universe, is a precursor of the modern consciousness that would no longer find meaning in the shattered heavens of religious certainty but in interpersonal relationships.

Love, however, was not the only way the poet had sought meaning. The young Donne was a man of insatiable ambition. Long before he became a preacher John Donne aspired to the highest stations in society. Yet his efforts at advancement were suspect because of his Roman Catholic origins. Therefore Donne had to find a way to prove his allegiance to the crown if he were ever to satisfy his hunger for worldly success.

In 1596, Donne saw his chance. He sailed with a military fleet under the command of the popular hero Earl of Essex. Essex was greatly favored by Queen Elizabeth, with whom he often played cards through the night. On June 21, 1596, a flotilla of British battleships, under the command of Essex and including John Donne in the company, launched an attack on Cadiz, Spain. They destroyed three warships and forty merchant ships. It was a terrifying scene: Donne witnessed the enemy sailors set on fire by the British artillery. He saw them plunging into the water where they were finished off by another barrage. The British went ashore and looted and razed the Spanish city.

As he lay dying, did Donne fill with sorrow at how thirty-five years earlier he had found in the death of others the hope of his own advancement? Beneath the God-shaped hole of his own age, Donne had gone asleep to the risen Christ, while he, like the Roman soldier on the sarcophagus, leaned upon the world's brutal power.

When Donne returned from his military exploits, his strategy for social advancement paid off handsomely. One of his fellow adventurers, Thomas Egerton, was knighted. His friend's father was Sir Thomas Egerton, the Lord Keeper, a powerful political figure in Queen Elizabeth's court. Sir Thomas Egerton's newly knighted son convinced his father to appoint John Donne as his secretary.

Thus by 1597 at the age of twenty-five John Donne had achieved an office of considerable social standing in court. As secretary to the Lord Keeper, Donne lived in the distinguished lodgings of York House, where the Lord Keeper made his home and where Donne rubbed shoulders with the rich and powerful. His military daring had paid off.

In 1601 Donne became a member of Parliament. He was now able to lease a royal grant of land and to write "Esquire" after his name. Success, oh sweet success! Donne rested on his accomplishments as securely as the soldier resting on his sword and sleeping through the resurrection. But then suddenly all that propped Donne up collapsed, and he was awakened to new realities.

He fell in love with a woman named Ann More. In an early letter he wrote her saying, "I thought thee an Angel at first sight." "Angel" turned out to be more than a romantic conceit. Ann was an angel in the classic biblical sense. She was a messenger who awakened the poet to the meaning and wonder of life that continue even when there is a God-shaped hole, even when the world is in fragments.

From the cloud Donne offers their marriage as a reminder to visionary preachers that human and divine love are often interfused in ways that we do not immediately perceive. It is through mortal love that the Spirit sometimes sighs most powerfully: "Follow the living Christ."

When they married in 1601, Ann More was seventeen and John Donne was twelve years her senior, twenty-nine. He had met her at York House. She was the daughter of George More, a wealthy landowner from Surrey. Donne and Ann were married secretly because Donne knew her father would not approve him as a partner in light of the poet's Catholic upbringing and his lack of a great fortune. Once the two were married, Donne planned to inform Ann's father at a propitious moment, hoping that George More would then welcome him into the family since the marriage was already an accomplished fact.

Things did not go as Donne had hoped. As soon as Ann's father found out about their union, he went into a rage. He demanded that Sir Thomas Egerton fire Donne from his position and put him in prison. George More tried to have his daughter's marriage annulled. But officials concluded that the marriage was legally binding and could not be invalidated.

Seeing that his daughter was now stuck with John Donne for better or worse, George More relented, and had Donne released from jail. He even tried to get Donne reinstated at court, but to no avail since Thomas Egerton and others with power and influence considered Donne's ill-advised marriage proof that he was untrustworthy. Never again would Donne rise as high in society and court as he had before his marriage. They lived hand to mouth for several years, depending upon the patronage and kindness of various friends.

They also began to have children, nearly one a year: Constance in 1603, John in 1604, George in 1605, Francis in 1607. The break in pregnancies can be traced to the fact that Donne traveled for a year in Europe with Sir Walter Chute, a trip that was part of his effort to get re-established in court.

But his efforts to reclaim a high position in society were to no avail. Upon his return, he and Ann moved to a house at Mitcham. Years later, when

Donne lay dying, he may have recalled the sad, impoverished days there. He may have smelled again the rank odor emitted from the basement and remembered how he struggled with depression and even considered committing suicide. Or perhaps he lifted his spirits with the memory of Ann and their utter and complete faithfulness to one another? For as the Donne scholar Derek Parker writes: "The marriage of John and Ann Donne is on the evidence we have one of the most ideal and complete in the history of the institution."[29]

In 1611, Donne, as part of his persistent efforts to re-establish his position in society, accompanied a nobleman to Europe. It was then that he wrote for his wife one of his most famous poems, "A Valediction: Forbidding Mourning." The poem was an attempt to quiet her distress at his departure. Later, when Donne was dying, I wonder if he recalled the poem, especially since the opening lines describe men dying:

> As virtuous men passe mildly away,
>   And whisper to their soules, to goe,
> Whilst some of their sad friends doe say,
>   The breath goes now, and some say, no:
>
> So let us melt, and make no noise,
>   No teare-floods, nor sigh-tempests move;
> 'Twere prophanation of our joyes
>   To tell the layetie our love. (p. 38)

Donne makes of Ann's and his love something sacred, a mystery that must not be profaned by exposure to those not initiated. He and his wife share in a priesthood of love which he contrasts to the more superficial relationships of most people, whom he designates "the layetie" and in a later stanza "Dull sublunary lovers." They are mundane folk who Donne says

> cannot admit
> Absence, because it doth remove
> Those things which elemented it.
>
> But we by a love, so much refin'd,
> That our selves know not what it is,
> Inter-assured of the mind,
> Care lesse, eyes, lips, and hands to misse.
>
> Our two soules therefore, which are one,
> Though I must goe, endure not yet
> A breach, but an expansion,
> Like gold to ayery thinnesse beate.

Did those words ring true to Donne, did they bring him comfort twenty years later when he was on his death bed, and as he recalled the other great partings of his life? In 1613 his son Nicholas died in infancy, in 1614 his daughter Mary and his son Francis died. And then in 1617 the saddest loss of his life: Ann died after her eleventh pregnancy, which ended in the delivery of a stillborn child. Donne was devastated by the loss. Some of the warmest, most personal lines in his poetry reflect the impact of her death. Holy Sonnet XVII opens:

> Since she whom I lov'd hath payd her last debt
> To Nature, and to hers, and my good is dead,
> And her Soule early into heaven ravished,
> Wholly on heavenly things my mind is sett. (p. 253)

Although Ann's death intensified Donne's attention to spiritual matters, he had in fact already been engaged in a process of transformation for some years. It would be a distortion to picture this process as a radical turning from his youthful ambition and passion to a life of piety. As with everything he did, save for his impetuous marriage, John Donne was always attentive to the social and economic ramifications of his actions. This is not to say that his increasing religious involvement was born of hypocrisy, for the motives of human beings, especially their religious motives, are seldom if ever completely pure and holy.

Visionary preachers do not live with the illusion of self-sanctity. They know that God alone is holy, and they have the grace to apply the hermeneutic of suspicion to their own utterances in the name of God. They hear Donne's story and instead of sitting in judgment, they reflect on their own entanglements, the twisted life processes through which they came awake to the living Christ.

In Donne's case, it became clear by the year 1614 that the way out of his impoverished state was to accept the only office that King James the First would offer him: ordination as an Anglican priest. Although years earlier Donne had renounced his Roman Catholicism, the idea of becoming a clergyman did not initially fit with his self-image. But finally, in January of 1615, John Donne was ordained.

Having acted as the king wished, Donne now had some leverage to pressure the king for appointment as a royal chaplain, a position which carried with it the possibility of a respectable personal income. Furthermore, the King commanded Cambridge University to make Donne a Doctor of Divinity. The faculty and administration were furious. They regarded Donne as nothing more than a conniving careerist who should never have been ordained in the first place. But the king and people in high places prevailed and Donne was honored with the Doctorate.

In the long run Donne would more than live up to the honor. For he was to become the most beloved preacher of his time and one of the most famous preachers in the English language. The living Christ has the power to make visionary preachers out of the most unlikely people once they have been awakened to resurrection. C. H. Sisson got it right when he concludes that Donne's life and work are a witness that

> the faith
> Is not exclusive in the fools its chooses
> That the vain, the ambitious and the highly sexed
> Are the natural prey of the incarnate Christ.

To this day people repeat and sing lines from John Donne, the preacher, which they may not realize come from a religious devotion that was penned nearly four hundred years ago:

> No man is an Iland, intire of it selfe; every man is a peece of the Continent, a part of the *maine*; if a *Clod* bee washed away by the *Sea*, *Europe* is the lesse, as well as if a *Promontorie* were . . . any mans *death* diminishes *me*, because I am involved in *Mankinde*; And therefore never send to know for whom the *bell* tolls; It tolls for *thee*. (p. 441)

Seven years after writing this, when Donne himself was dying, did these memorable words come back to him and bring some sense of what his loss would mean for those he left behind? Did he hear the echo of his own voice from when he used to preach to large crowds in the open air at St. Paul's cross? Were there faces, expressions, nods of approval from his listeners that came back to him now as his life faded? Retired preachers have often shared such memories with me so it seems reasonable that Donne would have similar recollections.

Perhaps he remembered when he was appointed to "Old Saint Paul's." This is not the church of the same name that now stands in London but rather a gothic building that would be destroyed in the great fire of 1666, thirty-five years after Donne died. Perhaps there echoed in the memory of the dying Donne the sound of the choir offering up an anthem, and perhaps the flow of remembered music gathered all of his memories into one great motion as a wave gathers out of the ocean, until it filled him with a surge of life so that he found the strength to repeat for one last time the bold lines of Holy Sonnet X:

Death be not proud, though some have called thee
Mighty and dreadfull, for thou art not soe,
For, those, whom thou think'st, thou dost overthrow,
Die not, poore death, nor yet canst thou kill me.
From rest and sleepe, which but thy pictures bee,
Much pleasure, then from thee, much more must flow,
And soonest our best men with thee doe goe,
Rest of their bones, and soules deliverie.
Thou art slave to Fate, Chance, kings, and desperate men,
And dost with poyson, warre, and sicknesse dwell,
And poppie, or charmes can make us sleepe as well,
And better than thy stroake; why swell'st thou then?
One short sleepe past, wee wake eternally,
And death shall be no more; death, thou shalt die.
   (pp. 250-51)

Was Donne this brave at the very end? The sonnet is not typical of most of his religious verse. It is brazen and confident in tone whereas most of his verse reveals a person struggling for faith. This is why his poetry is instructive for those who preach while the church is under reconstruction. Through Donne we gain a vision of the heart wrestling with its own inadequacies in a fragmented age. In one of his most famous sonnets, Holy Sonnet XIV, Donne pictures the soul as a walled city, a fortress resisting the entrance of God:

Batter my heart, three person'd God; for, you
As yet but knocke, breathe, shine, and seeke to mend;
That I may rise, and stand, o'erthrow mee, and bend
Your force, to break, blowe, burn and make me new.
   (p. 252)

Perhaps, then, Donne was not so brave as to recite "Death be not proud" upon his death bed. Maybe his spirit in the closing hours was closer to his hymn about the search for ultimate reconciliation and peace with the divine, "A Hymn to God the Father."

Although the hymn expresses a struggle common to many believers and seekers, it is also a profoundly personal statement. The poet has built into the poem a continual play upon his name, through the repeated use of the verb "done," meaning "accomplished" or "finished." The pun in the repeated phrase "thou hast not *done*" means simultaneously two different things: "you, O God, have not finished or completed your task," *and* "you, O God, do not yet have me or possess me, John Donne, as your own."

Perhaps then on that final day, March 31, 1631, John Donne ended his search for meaning in a fragmented age by knowing in his soul what he affirms in this great hymn:

I

Wilt thou forgive that sinne where I begunne,
    Which is my sin, though it were done before?
Wilt thou forgive those sinnes, through which I runne,
    And do run still: though still I do deplore?
    When thou hast done, thou hast not done,
        For, I have more.

II

Wilt thou forgive that sinne by which I'have wonne
    Others to sinne? and, made my sinne their doore?
Wilt thou forgive that sin which I did shunne
    A yeare, or two: but wallowed in, a score?
    When thou hast done, thou hast not done,
        For I have more.

III

I have a sinne of feare, that when I have spunne
    My last thred, I shall perish on the shore;
Sweare by thy selfe, that at my death thy sonne
    Shall shine as he shines now, and heretofore;
    And, having done that, Thou hast done,
        I feare no more.[30]

EXTRAVAGANT PASSION AND INTEGRATIVE IMAGINATION

It took Donne his full life to come to the point that he could claim, "Thou hast done, / I feare no more." He found the true cross and the living Christ. Even if our route to that destination is less circuitous than Donne's, his life is a reminder of what a rigorous undertaking it is to find our way faithfully through a world of broken meaning.

Despite his foibles and failures, Donne possessed two qualities that made him a visionary preacher of extraordinary power. First, he never denied or lost touch with his humanity. There was a full-blooded passion about the man that earlier in his life led him to "wallow" in sin, but that later gave his preaching urgency, creative daring, and power. In his poem "A Letter to John Donne" C. H. Sisson contrasts Donne's animal vitality with a preacher who has confused becoming passionless with piety:

> You brought body and soul to this church
> Walking there through the park alive with deer
> But now what animal has climbed into your pulpit?
> One whose pretension is that the fear
> Of God has heated him into a spirit
> An evaporated man no physical ill can hurt.
>
> Well might you hesitate at the Latin gate
> Seeing such apes denying the church of God:
> I am grateful particularly that you were not a saint
> But extravagant whether in bed or in your shroud.
> You would understand that in the presence of folly
> I am not sanctified but angry.[31]

Donne's example reminds us that visionary preaching is more than an intellectual quest. It involves our whole being, the giving of ourselves with extravagant passion to life, to love, to God.

The other quality that made Donne a great

visionary preacher was his ceaseless effort to piece together the meaning of life. He never gave up on this no matter how fragmented the world or his personal circumstances. In poem and sermon alike he risked one astonishing image after another. He tried to find the connections between seemingly contradictory realities. He made audacious leaps of the imagination to draw constellations of meaning between religion, literature, politics, science, and global exploration. Instead of running away from the God-shaped hole of his fragmented age, he faced it and threw his imaginative energies into creating a body of poems and sermons that still grip us with their daring, their insight, their faithfulness to the living God.

By the end of his life, Donne had moved from the posture of the Roman soldier leaning on the sword to the posture of the faithful figure open to the mystery of the risen Christ. Donne became a visionary preacher in a church and a world under reconstruction. The extravagance of his passions fueled the courage of his imagination so that his witness to God pulsed with an intellectual, emotional energy that could inspire a church under reconstruction. And it is to the exercise of that same extravagant passion and imaginative courage that we are called by the Spirit who sighs:

Keep awake to the resurrection.
Follow the living Christ.

Chapter 4

The Spirit Sighs:
Expand and Enlighten the
Landscape of the Heart

FROM AN INVERTED BOWL TO
GLOBULAR CLUSTERS

I look up through the God-shaped hole to see stars and a sliver of moon. Words drift through my mind, witnesses whispering to me in the silence:

> I see your handiwork
> in the heavens:
> the moon and the stars
> you set in place. (Psalm 8:3)[1]

I think of ancient Hebrew cosmology and look up the word "firmament" in a Bible dictionary. The biblical writers pictured the sky as "a domed expanse of heavens holding back celestial waters from terrestrial. The Hebrew term *raqia'* suggests a thin sheet of beaten metal."[2] A line drawing of the ancient cosmos accompanies the article. The dome of heaven looks like an inverted bowl resting over the earth, which itself has the appearance of a pie plate. The picture is so utterly alien to modern scientific thought that I am moved to search out my *National Geographic Atlas* and study its maps of the universe: cylindrical cross sections of galaxies are printed in midnight blue against a black background. The copy in the margins begins with a general reflection: "My suspicion is that the universe is not only queerer than we suppose, but queerer than we *can* suppose."[3] If a God-shaped hole with a cloud of witnesses seems a bit of wild imagining, just look at the night sky: God has the wildest imagination of all. Our galaxy

> is only one of billions of galaxies. It is a gravitationally bound, rotating congregation of hundreds of billions of stars. The central bulge glows with the light of older, redder stars. Globular clusters contain the galaxy's oldest stars—estimated at 10 to 15 billion years. Gas and dust condensing in the spiral arms are even now forming new stars.[4]

As I read these words, I sense the cloud of witnesses is gathered around me, but they do not want to block the view of the universe so they content themselves with speaking in my heart. Even Galileo joins with the doctors of the church who once condemned him to exclaim: "Reality is infinitely more vast and wonderful than any of us thought."

I leave the Bible dictionary and the atlas open on my desk and look alternately at the inverted bowl of the biblical firmament and the cylindrical cross sections of galaxies. The biblical dome of heaven is more than a picture of an antiquated cosmology. It maps a landscape in the heart where everything is ordered and contained. It pictures a way of understanding our place in creation which, no matter how helpful to ancient believers, is now inadequate.

I turn from the dome of heaven to study closely the

ever expanding universe. The more I read and study the pictures, the more my heart fills with wonder. The new cosmology awakens in me the rhapsodic spirit of the psalmist. I join the psalmist in exclaiming:

> I see your handiwork
> in the heavens:
> the moon and the stars
> you set in place.

Yet when I recite these words before the image of the expanding universe, they strike me as too static for a visionary preacher who is called to speak of God in the coming millennium. They suggest a God who hangs the stars in space as we hang a chandelier from the ceiling or ornaments from a Christmas tree. The psalm does not do justice to the dynamism of the universe, to the explosion of matter that scattered into billions of galaxies with billions of stars. I share the rapture of the psalmist, but the language and cosmology of the psalmist are no longer a fully satisfactory expression of why I am filled with wonder.

The tension between the inverted bowl and the cylindrical maps of the universe creates an opening in my consciousness. I look up through the God-shaped hole in the church under reconstruction and with a rush of wind, the Spirit sighs: "Expand and enlighten the landscape of the heart."

THE WAY THE WORLD IS
IS THE WAY THE WORLD IS NOT

Many years ago I had a student who, until she came to the Northeast for her theological education, had spent her entire life in a landscape I had never visited: the desert Southwest of the United

137

States. I had grown up in upstate New York, on a mountain lake surrounded by green fields and dense woods, not far from where I would serve as a pastor and later teach in seminary.

During the student's first spring in the Northeast, she felt suffocated by the trees that were leafing out because they obscured her view of the sky. She did not know how we who were natives of the region could bear to live in such a thickly shaded environment. To her it did not seem "natural."

A few years later I visited this student in the desert where she had returned for her ordination. I was astounded by the barrenness of the place: nothing but cacti, sand, and rock. I did not know how the natives of the region could live in such an arid, treeless environment. Riding through an especially desolate stretch of road. I said to her: "You live on a different planet here." She responded: "No, you're the one who lives on a different planet." She stopped the car and started showing me small insects and animals, cacti with flowers whose petals are arranged to funnel morning dew to the plant, others with roots that spread out a mile from the trunk in order to gather every last drop of moisture available. Her dead planet was teeming with life!

We carry with us the landscape where we were born and raised. And what is true of our geographic experience is also true of our spiritual life, of the way we envision God, creation, and the meaning of faith. We each have our peculiar "landscape of the heart." I take the phrase from the Australian poet James McAuley, who, in a poem that explains why he is a Christian poet, makes the following appeal to fellow poets:

> Scorn then to darken and contract
> The landscape of the heart
> By individual, arbitrary
> And self-expressive art.[5]

McAuley's exhortation applies to visionary preachers as well as to poets. We are not "to darken and contract / The landscape of the heart."

Far too much preaching has done that in the past. Again and again we have heard the cloud weeping as witnesses from the past have come to realize how constricted their vision was. They assumed that their experience of the world defined what the world is.

The task of visionary preachers is not to darken and contract, but to enlighten and expand the landscape of the heart, to broaden the capacity of human beings to extend the grace and compassion of God to others.

The landscape of the heart is the world of meaning that a community constructs out of its stories, rituals, symbols, beliefs, and values. Although the landscape of each human being's heart has its unique features, it is predominantly a socially constructed and shared landscape. The repeated actions and words of the communities that raise us plant our inner worlds with symbols and values and create a landscape where we feel at home.

The Hebrew worshipers who repeated the words of the psalmist,

> I see your handiwork
> in the heavens:
> the moon and the stars
> you set in place

felt at home beneath the inverted bowl of the firmament.

To expand and enlighten the landscape of the heart is hard work. Just as my student and I were astounded by our different natural environments, so too, religious people find it difficult to comprehend landscapes of the heart that are different from what they have known and experienced. An unfamiliar landscape often appears as dead to us as the desert did to me, when in fact it teems with life. Even within the same society the landscape of the heart can vary from individual to individual, and from congregation to congregation. These differences are frequently the source of religious and theological conflict. If preachers do not understand the landscape of the heart that defines a particular congregation's understanding, then their preaching may fail.

CAPTURING THE IMAGINATION FOR GOD

Leonora Tubbs Tisdale gives preachers tools for understanding the landscape of a congregation's heart. Drawing upon anthropology, congregational studies, and her own experience of preaching in different contexts, she describes how effective preachers present a theology that is

> seriously imaginable to a particular people in a particular time and place. The term "seriously imaginable" involves possibilities that are both "real"—as opposed to mere fantasy—and "for us"—that is, imaginable within the particular social world a people inhabit.[6]

If preaching is to reach any group of people they must find in the sermon some connection to the landscape of their hearts, to the world of stories, symbols, values, and rituals that give meaning to their existence. To do this is to achieve a "seriously imaginable" theology, that is to say, a theology that makes sense of the listeners' lives, that brings meaning to the joys and tragedies of their existence, that gives them power to live out the values of the gospel.

The complexity of achieving a "seriously imaginable" theology lies in the fact that the gospel of Christ does not confirm or reinforce everything in the landscape of the heart of any culture or religious group. The gospel often challenges what we hold in our hearts, particularly those prejudices that lead to the devaluation and destruction of human beings.

Visionary preachers are stretched between the needs of communication and transformation. Communication requires connection to the landscape of the heart. Transformation requires expanding and enlightening the landscape. Visionary preachers move back and forth between the two as a way of "capturing the imagination" for God.[7]

Preachers often think of "capturing the imagination" as little more than a communication strategy to get a congregation's attention. We look for an opening story or a lively phrase that will "pique people's interest." But this superficial assessment undervalues the power of "capturing the imagination." Advertisers and politicians understand that the way to sell a product or a candidate is to capture people's imagination, to gain entrance into the way they organize the world. The appeal through the electronic media is not simply to our reason, but to the landscape of our hearts. Commercials and advertisements tell us again and again that one's value as a person is a function of what one possesses: the car one drives, the house one owns, the athletic shoes one wears.

The global economy is now working to capture the imagination of the whole world with a vision for the need to acquire its products. Although there may be some gains worthy of our support in a world economy, there are also values and systems of exploitation that are in direct conflict with the values of what God envisions for the human family. Here is an aboriginal poet of Australia warning about these culturally destructive possibilities:

Child, leave the tape recorder
and video alone. It will make
your eyes go very sore if you
look and look at it all the time.

Play the music a bit low,
or else, your ears will explode
from listening to it.

Leave cigarettes alone or they
might burn you and another thing
is, leave the grog alone too.
You might make yourself sick.
Be good!

Leave the White man's things
music, grog, cigarettes, video
and those other things as well!

Come to the ceremonies
come hunting and dancing,
come, so that you can know your
own culture.[8]

The poet realizes the importance of capturing the imagination for holy purposes. She understands the spiritual dangers posed by the global economy: how it threatens to corrode and negate the world of meaning that has sustained her people. She exhorts her child, "Come to the ceremonies / come hunting and dancing," because she knows these rituals supply a friendly environment for the religious imagination, for the landscape of the heart that her community treasures.

RECONSTRUCTING THE CHURCH AS A FRIENDLY ENVIRONMENT FOR THE IMAGINATION

Wherever I travel, preachers tell me that they want to preach with a livelier imagination, but many are afraid to do so. They are afraid because seminary professors and other authority figures have warned against being "too imaginative," of "diluting the gospel." They are afraid because there are people in their congregations who will bully them with quotations from the Bible. They are afraid because they are haunted by the vision of an angry deity who will judge them for abandoning his word. (The masculine possessive is deliberate: the fear is of a furious father.) They are afraid because the church is a hostile environment for the imagination.

At the naming of these fears, the cloud of witnesses gathers in the God-shaped hole and looks down with compassion upon the preachers of the earth. Without judgment or condescension, the witnesses tell how they lived with the same fears in their day and age. If only they had known then what they know now, they would never have allowed such fears to rule them. God is a freer Spirit than mortal flesh has ever imagined. The excesses of a visionary preacher, if they lead people to love and serve God, are more faithful to the Spirit than heavy-handed theology that makes God inaccessible.

Preachers seeking to win the human imagination for God need an environment friendly to the imagination, friendly to the visionary powers that are a gift of the Spirit. Preachers can nurture that environment by doing three things:

- immersing themselves in the conventional imagination of the community
- naming the power and limitations of the conventional imagination
- maintaining openness to possibilities that have never occurred to the conventional imagination.

By "conventional imagination" I mean the landscape of the heart that has been shaped by the cloud of witnesses and the peculiarities of local tradition.[9] It is the mind-set which prevails in the congregation as a whole, their *Weltanschauung*. It is the character of their group life, their values and symbols, their way of being church, their way of relating to the larger Christian tradition and the world.

Each strategy for reconstructing the church as an environment friendly to the imagination puts in action a classical Christian doctrine. When we immerse ourselves in the community's imagination, we recapitulate the pattern of *incarnation*. When we name the power and limitations of the conventional imagination, we carry on the church's historical task of *reinterpreting tradition*. When we open ourselves to possibilities that the conventional imagination cannot even see, we prepare ourselves to receive the flame and wind of *Pentecost*. Visionary preaching flows from an imagination alive to the new meanings of the core affirmations and stories of faith.

- Visionary preaching, like Christ, is incarnational.
- Visionary preaching, like Christ, reinterprets tradition.
- Visionary preaching, like Christ, breathes with the Spirit.

INCARNATION

The prologue to the Gospel of John proclaims: "The *logos* [word] became *sarx* [flesh] and dwelt among us" (John 1:14). I have given preference to the two Greek words because the English translations fail to do justice to the richness of the original language.

Logos means more than "word." *Logos* includes the wisdom and creative power of God that is greater than language. *Logos* is a term with both Greek philosophical and biblical roots, a way of expressing "the mode of divine creativity and revelation."[10] The *logos* of God was active long before humans spoke their first syllable. Everything that exists has been made through the *logos*.

As *logos* means more than "word" so *sarx* means more than "flesh." *Sarx* embraces the sum total of what constitutes being human. *Sarx* includes the conventionally imagined world, the landscapes of meaning that communities plant in the heart of their people through prayer and ritual, symbol and action, music and story.

When we confine *logos* to language, to "word," we are apt to assume that God requires that others talk our talk and walk our walk. Moving to a new church we are often puzzled by the distinctive customs and rituals of the congregation. Because they do not conform to our way of speaking and acting we are not able to grasp how the *logos* becomes *sarx* through their way of life. But before visionary preachers make any attempt at changing a congregation's peculiar practices, they enter the landscape of the heart that holds these things to be precious. They attempt to understand how the practices of the congregation may be the *logos* becoming *sarx* for this particular people.

A former colleague in homiletics used to tell his students that when they moved to a new church they should treat the congregation and its customs with the same respect they would show upon entering someone else's house for a meal. No decent guest would arrive to criticize the arrangement of the furniture, the pictures hanging on the walls, and the food that was served. A good guest is eager to hear the story behind an old family heirloom and why a certain picture holds such meaning and how the recipe for the main dish has been passed down through the generations.

Preachers are guests in a household of faith that has seen preachers come and go, and they need to honor the ways of that household before they attempt any change. Not always, but sometimes the church is a hostile environment for the imagination of the preacher because the preacher is hostile to the imagination of the church, to the landscape of the heart that prevails in the congregation.

When preachers immerse themselves in the imagined worlds of their congregations, they are recapitulating the pattern and principle of Christ's incarnation, of *logos* becoming *sarx*: they give expression to what it means to embody the word in a particular time and place.

When we lose the wealth of associations evoked by *logos* and *sarx* we fall into a disembodied understanding of the gospel. We reduce faith to a word game, a theological crossword puzzle. We expect from the interpretation of texts more than language alone can deliver. We forget that our experience as creatures of muscle and bone has dimensions that language can evoke but never capture. For example, reading manuals about pregnancy is not the same as bearing a child and giving birth. As helpful as scholars are in providing background and knowledge about the Scriptures, exegesis plus hermeneutics does not equal a sermon, does not equal the embodiment of the truth that sounds in the overtones of the preacher's voice and dances in gesture and facial expression:

> If we assign the purely cognitive transposition a determining role, we cause great damage, not merely to the text but to us the hearers and to the society that must live with the questions. For if we miss the complementary emotional and somatic particles, we miss the whole. The conviction that conflicts of interpretation

are solved by rational debate is wishful thinking to a terrifying degree, and with disastrous results.[11]

The "disastrous results" are religious warfare in the church and society. Different factions claim to be "biblical" while they charge that their opponents are not. Using a "purely cognitive transposition" from the text to our situation today, the combatants create an environment hostile to the imagination. They are baffled by visionary preaching because it refuses to participate in the "wishful thinking" that "rational debate" will settle theological conflict.

The imagination of visionary preachers draws on "complementary emotional and somatic particles" that are rooted in the materiality and culture of a particular congregation. Despite our technologically interconnected world, despite the global commercialization of McDonalds and Kentucky Fried Chicken, despite mass media pop figures, churches are still amazingly local phenomena. The realities that give meaning to life are as geographically specific and incarnate as the child born to a woman named Mary in Bethlehem in the days of Caesar Augustus:

> The development of local theologies depends as much on finding Christ already active in the culture as it does on bringing Christ to the culture. The great respect for culture has a christological basis. It grows out of a belief that the risen Christ's salvific activity in bringing about the kingdom of God is already going on before our arrival.[12]

There are traps in taking locality and embodiment seriously. We may preach to please. Our sermons may become "prey to a cultural romanticism, unable to see the sin in its own historical experience."[13] No wonder the cloud of witnesses is essential. Without their tears and wisdom, "a local church runs the risk of turning in on itself, becoming self-

147

satisfied with its own achievements."[14] And there is another risk as well: we can become as arrogant about our failures as our achievements. We may think no one else has ever suffered as we have. Concluding that we are the first community of faith to live with a God-shaped hole, we cut ourselves off from the wisdom of our ancestors in the cloud who faced their own theological fragmentation. The church under reconstruction at its best is

a complex of those cultural patterns in which the gospel has taken on flesh, at once enmeshed in the local situation, extending through communities in our own time and in the past, and reaching out to the eschatological realization of the fullness of God's reign.[15]

When visionary preachers draw upon all these dimensions to provide glimpses of grace and meaning, then God and the gospel become "seriously imaginable" in the community's life. Their sermons enable the congregation to live faithfully in a fragmented age. The *logos* becomes *sarx* here and now.

TRADITION

The cloud gathers in the God-shaped hole and begins to sing a hymn that embodies the theological daring of a visionary preacher/poet who has entered the landscape of a people's heart to give witness to the *logos* becoming *sarx*:

'Twas in the moon of wintertime,
when all the birds had fled,
that mighty Gitchi Manitou
sent angel choirs instead;
before their light the stars grew dim,
and wondering hunters heard the hymn:

Jesus your King is born,
Jesus is born,
in excelsis gloria.

Within a lodge of broken bark
the tender babe was found;
a ragged robe of rabbit skin
enwrapped his beauty round;
but as the hunter braves drew nigh,
the angel song rang loud and high:

Jesus your King is born,
Jesus is born,
in excelsis gloria.[16]

I conjure up an image of an infant in "a ragged robe of rabbit skin" and notice how utterly different it is from the silhouette of the Almighty Father that has collapsed to leave the God-shaped hole. A fresh wind blows through the opening, and out of the cloud there marches a procession of artists who carry astoundingly varied images of the nativity. There are Japanese silk screens with kimono-clad Madonnas, Northern European medieval block prints featuring shepherds in cowls and a stable of crumbling walls, Italian Renaissance palaces with rich velvet drapes and the Magi kneeling on marbled floors, Latin American paintings with thatched roof barns surrounded by shepherds in blue jeans who emerge from tropical rain forests, Rembrandt etchings with a chubby infant and a round-faced mother, southwestern Indian paintings that feature midnight blue skies and visitors arriving on horses with colorful beaded bridles and reins . . .

The procession of images is creating a friendly environment for the imagination. The cloud is reminding us of both the power and the limitation of the conventional imagination. The power is the ability to create vivid images, to present "seriously imaginable" visions of the *logos* becoming *sarx*. The limitation is to believe that our particular images are full, final, and adequate.

The parade in the cloud reveals that tradition is not a closed treasure chest but a continuous

149

process of reinterpretation and reimagining. The parade leader is Christ, who in the Gospels is constantly reinterpreting tradition. Consider, for example, his conflicts with the authorities over the Sabbath. Christ uses a dynamic understanding of tradition to correct its misuse: the Sabbath was made for human beings, not human beings for the Sabbath. Reinterpretation opens the landscape of the heart to the new work of God.

Reinterpretation does not end with Jesus. The procession of images from the weeping, singing, praying, preaching cloud is a witness to the dynamism of tradition. The procession includes more than the graphic work of artists. The church's worship and song through the ages reveals a perpetual shift in the images of God and humanity. Lionel Adey summarizes the history of western hymnody as the transformation of the Christian myth through the centuries, a transformation that resonated in the sermons and homilies of preachers:

> Our study of the Myth in hymns has recorded an evolution from human passivity as a Heavenly King puts to flight the rebel angel (or serpent or dragon) responsible for man's expulsion from Paradise to a passionate identification with that Redeemer in his lowly birth and cruel death; from awe before the God who has descended for man's redemption to a love of Jesus that alternated with a fear of Christ the Judge so intense as to make death more terrifying than if believed final; from a retelling of the *mythos* or "sacred history" to a defining of the Spirit's operation within the heart, or a connecting of personal misdeeds with the "sins of the world" for which Christ died.[17]

The procession of images flows through plainsong and chant, hymn and chorale, doxology and lament, carol and praise chorus. By music and song the cloud motions for us to join the parade, to continue the task of reinterpretation in our own day. The wind sweeps us into the procession and encourages us to take up what the earlier marchers have left behind: "Just as a literary critic tries to interpret a poem or a novel in such a way as to return the reader to a deeper experience of the work of art, so the theologian [or visionary preacher] tries to interpret an imagistic tradition in order to renew its religious potential."[18]

The "imagistic tradition" reminds us that the imagination required for visionary preaching is not pure fancy. It is not creation *ex nihilo*. The cloud is a major source of ideas and energy for expanding and enlightening the landscape of the heart: "Tradition, then, cannot be rejected but must be reconstructed with a view to what people can accept as expressive reality. Imagination, therefore, can be free or rule governed; in the case of theology, it should be the latter."[19]

PENTECOST

At this last sentence a fierce gale of Wind blasts through the God-shaped hole to protest the false choice of exercising a "free" or "rule governed" imagination. *Both* are essential to visionary preaching. A theology that does not allow for the "free" imagination is closed to the surprising work of the Spirit, closed to Pentecost, closed to what lies beyond the bounds of the conventional imagination. The denial of the free imagination leads to a shriveled landscape of the heart, to a heart that does not know the joy of rhapsodic prayer, the moment of wonder and holy splendor, the sweep of the Wind, the weeping and the singing of the cloud. Visionary preachers realize that "at its most authentic the visionary experience illuminates what is excellent in the world without excluding or denying what is bad."[20]

151

Visionary preachers oscillate between freedom and rules, between rhapsody and reason.[21] They trace out the principles of their experience but do not let this "rule governed" work imprison them or their preaching. Free imagination keeps the rules from making visionary preachers stagnant. "Rule governed" imagination keeps free imagination from making visionary preachers incoherent. Visionary preachers realize that the moment of transfigured consciousness and creative insight will make no sense unless they create a sermon structure that others can follow. Visionary preachers understand that "Form is the only bucket that will bring up what's in the Muses' well,"[22] what's in the Spirit's depths.

The visionary imagination is a Pentecostal imagination: free enough to receive the Spirit (Acts 2:1-13), structured enough to declare the meaning of the Spirit's presence (Acts 2:14-36). Pentecost reveals that there are possibilities within us far greater than our conventional imaginations allow. Who would ever have picked Peter, that wavering and unreliable disciple, to deliver the first major sermon after the ascension of Christ? Yet there he stands before a crowd enlightening and expanding the landscape of the heart: "In the last days it will be, God declares, that I will pour out my Spirit upon all flesh, and your sons and your daughters shall prophesy, and your young men shall see visions and your old men shall dream dreams" (Acts 2:17, quoting Joel 2:28 in a modified form).

THE POLYPHONIC SPIRIT OF GOD

Peter's Pentecost sermon sounds anew in the church under reconstruction, and I look up through the God-shaped hole to catch the vision of a sculpture I saw many years ago at the entrance to the harbor of Vlissingen, Holland. Standing on a promontory, the sculpture consisted of scores of pipes, each a different length and diameter. They were set at various angles and directions to catch the different winds that blew. Each pipe emitted its own unique pitch and tonal quality, though all of them had a flutelike, hollow sound, similar to what you can produce by blowing across the top of an empty soda bottle. At the dying and rising of the wind, the pitches and tones would change. At the shifting of the wind's direction some pipes fell silent while others became more prominent, depending on how they were angled. And sometimes, when the wind pattern was disturbed by the passing of a great ship or the localized gusts off strand and bay, there was a subtle polyphony: pipes making crescendos and decrescendos independently of one another.

Ever since that trip, I have listened to the wind in the trees and the chimney and the screen doors and windows of my home with an attentiveness I never before gave to those sounds. How different each one is: the trees swoosh, the chimney oofs, the screens whistle. The Vlissingen pipes awakened me to an awareness of the wind's music in my common surroundings.

Visionary preaching is like that sculpture: it awakens us to hear the various pitches and timbres of the Spirit sounding through the landscape of the heart. We develop a Pentecostal imagination so that we are able to hear the Wind of the Spirit sounding in multiple ways through different people and their varied ways of expressing the truth of God. (Cf. Acts 2:4-11.) We come to know the Spirit of God as a polyphonic Spirit.

At the mention of the polyphonic Spirit, the great

poet/preacher John Donne appears again in the cloud. But this time, instead of preaching or reciting his poetry, Donne beckons another witness, the English renaissance composer Thomas Tallis (c. 1505–1585). Tallis composed the music that later became the setting for the beloved hymn "All Praise to Thee, My God, This Night."[23] Donne, who often worshiped to Tallis's music, asks the composer to lead the cloud in singing another one of his most popular works, "If Ye Love Me," an anthem which continues to be in the repertoire of many church choirs.

While the cloud sings the great polyphonic anthem, I imagine the people who sat in the pews the first time the piece was sung during a service. England was reeling from the impact of the continental reformations that had torn a God-shaped hole in the church of the Middle Ages. There was a mean spirit in the air. Cruel. Vicious. Intolerant. It often broke into violence. England was soaked in the most incendiary kind of intellectual kerosene: theologically reinforced politics and politically reinforced theology. It was one of those eras which gives meaning to a comment by Mahatma Gandhi which a friend once recounted to me. The great Indian leader was asked, "What do you think of Western civilization?" Gandhi answered: "It would be a good idea."

Among the big players in England during the 1500s were King Henry VIII, desperate to have a male heir to the throne, followed by Edward VI, then Mary Stewart, and after her Queen Elizabeth I. They are the ones who make the historical novels and movies. Henry the Eighth getting fatter and fatter, prison, torture, and beheadings—they all make for lively drama and vivid cinema.

Thomas Tallis is not nearly so promising a figure for Hollywood as any of those famous public personages. He was born some time around 1505 and lived to 1585. He died of natural causes—a considerable achievement considering that he served all four monarchs!

As I listen to "If Ye Love Me," I keep thinking of the ordinary churchgoers who continued to attend services during those tumultuous times. Amidst the theological and political uproar, the serene beauty of Tallis's music must have been a moment of blessed peace for them. There are witnesses in the cloud who can remember what it was like. They had grown up in church, attending what was called the "Sarum Rite."

The word "Sarum" is the Latin word for the English Salisbury. Salisbury Cathedral had a central role in the development of worship in English churches. Sometime around 1100 c.e., English worshipers had begun to modify the Roman ritual at the Cathedral of Salisbury. The modifications fit the landscape of the English heart so well that the Rite of Sarum became the way people worshiped throughout England, and the prayers of Sarum were deeply beloved. They defined the conventional imagination of the believers. So it is not far-fetched to imagine worshipers who gathered during the tumult of the 1500s and who remembered with affection a less troubled time of faith when their parents taught them to pray from a Sarum book of hours:

God be in my head and in my understanding,
God be in my eyes and in my looking,
God be in my mouth and in my speaking,
God be in my heart and in my thinking,
God be at my end and my departing.
Amen

How they must have longed for those simpler, earlier days of faith before the church was under reconstruction. But now I picture them entering the

155

church in 1562. Three years ago the Act of Settlement was passed, which wiped out the Book of Sarum. People are no longer to worship according to the rite with which they were raised. I see them filing into their pews and bringing with them all the concerns that human beings have brought generation after generation to church: a prayer for their child who is sick, a prayer for the neighbor down the street who is having a hard time of it, a prayer for a mother who has died, a prayer for their own befuddled souls, a prayer for the world.

All their supplications gather to a prayer too deep for words, the sighing of the Spirit in their wearied souls: "O my God, where is peace, where is healing?" They are exhausted by the conflicted words of the age, by the different factions who claim to possess the truth of God and who damn to hell anyone who opposes them. But then the choir stands and sings Thomas Tallis's "If Ye Love Me" and the God-shaped hole fills with the cloud and the Wind lifts their hearts with hope.

In the silence that follows the music, the worshipers in the church under reconstruction suddenly realize that they have heard God speak with a profundity that all the politicians and theologians have missed. The Spirit has spoken to them through polyphonic music.

When Tallis first started writing church music earlier in the 1500s, he had composed what is called homophonic music. It had a single melodic line, sometimes in unison, sometimes lightly embroidered with harmony. But, just as the currents of theological and political intrigue crossed the channel into England, so too did new developments in music, including polyphony. Instead of a single melody there were multiple melodies all going on separately yet at the same time interweaving to create a gorgeous structure. Tallis took up this new musical idiom in his own compositions.

The worshipers who first heard "If Ye Love Me" now gather in the cloud above me and confirm the truth that they dimly sensed on earth when Tallis's music brought peace to their troubled hearts. The music reveals that God is a polyphonic Spirit who sings and speaks in multiple ways. The worshipers weep to imagine how different their brutal age would have been if crown and church had known that God was a polyphonic Spirit. Instead of reinforcing political torture and execution with theology, they might have heard the Spirit sighing in different timbres and pitches, like the pipes at Vlissingen, like the interweaving melodies of Tallis's music.

The cloud looks down through the God-shaped hole and wonders if we who now worship in the church under reconstruction will have a faith mature enough to recognize that God sings as a polyphonic Spirit through multiple cultures and ways of being. Hearing their question in my heart brings back a personal story of moving from belief in a homophonic God to a polyphonic Spirit.

When I was growing up, I sometimes attended church with my junior high girlfriend. One Sunday the sermon was so interesting that she and I whispered about it during the service. When I came home, my mother called to me, "Thomas Henry Troeger." The use of my full name was a clear sign that something was amiss. I walked into the kitchen, and she said to me: "You don't talk in church. Ever."

"Mom, it was about the sermon."

"You don't talk in church."

"But, Mom, we were . . ."

"You don't talk in church."

"But . . ."

157

"You don't talk in church."

This was rural upstate New York, a white Presbyterian church.

The story did not end in the kitchen with my mother saying, "You don't talk in church." It continued many years later when I was in seminary and attended for the first time in my life an African American Baptist service. Starting with the opening prayer, people in the congregation were saying "Amen," and "Please, Lord," and "Yes, Jesus." I was nearly moved to get up and say, "You don't talk in church." But I did not because my childhood church, the church of the silent congregation, also taught me that a Christian respects other people, their different ways, their different faiths. That is part of what it means to show the love of Christ. So I sat there and listened to the chorus of responses throughout the service and sermon. And I kept going to those services until I enjoyed the congregational response so much that I joined in myself.

Several years later I was teaching in seminary and participating in the ordination of one of my former students. The clergy had all gathered in an education room of an upstate New York, white Presbyterian church to say a prayer before service. While somebody was leading the prayer, I unconsciously started saying, "Yes, Jesus. Amen. Thank you. Please come." All of a sudden I was aware everyone was looking at me. Their faces all asked the same question: What has gotten into you?

The polyphonic Spirit of God!

While the cloud of witnesses sings Tallis's interweaving melodies, I think of the "culture wars," the debates about pluralism that resound in society and in the church under reconstruction. The polyphonic music from the cloud warns us not to enforce a unison theology, as though God only sings homophonic music, only speaks in one language, only acts in one way. Did the Spirit move in that white upstate Presbyterian congregation that never stirred or made a sound except for the singing of the hymns, the recitation of the creed, and the unison prayers? Yes. And did the Spirit move through those African American Baptist services with the congregation talking back to the preacher and clapping their hands and swaying their bodies? Yes. In each case it was the polyphonic Spirit, the God who refuses to be confined to homophonic theology. Like Tallis's interweaving, independent melodies, like the shifting winds through the pipes at Vlissingen, the Spirit moves at multiple speeds in every direction through all kinds of witnesses.

The voices of the cloud borne on the Wind plead with us not to replace the polyphonic Spirit with homophonic theology. For if we do, we will continue the horrifying history of religious conflict fed by the illusion that the Spirit moves in a single direction with a single voice. The task of us visionary preachers who worship in the church under reconstruction is not to fill in the God-shaped hole with another image, since whatever we place there will be inadequate. The task of visionary preachers is to enlighten and expand the landscape of the heart, to honor the polyphonic Spirit in her plurality of manifestations, in his multiplicity of revelations.

We still treasure particular images and understandings of God, the Creator hovering over the deep, the *logos* becoming *sarx* in Jesus Christ, the Spirit as flame and wind. We still preach sermons that reflect the peculiarities of our local culture and congregation. But we do all of this understanding that we are part of the cloud of witnesses that does not sing in unison but in polyphony. Just as sopranos and altos, tenors and basses have different ranges and degrees of vocal agility, so too we have our unique gifts and limits. No one preacher, no one church, no one religion can sing every part. This is what the cloud of witnesses has come to see by the grace of God and the congregated light of the ages. This broad ecumenical and interreligious perspective is not a watering down of Christian belief but an intensification and expansion of faith that is responsive to the polyphonic Spirit.

There are preacher/poets in the church under reconstruction who are already beginning to live the truth that sounds in the cloud and blows on the Wind. The Guatemalan poet and theologian Julia Esquivel, who has survived decades of brutal war, acknowledges that "In this land God cannot be represented by one religion." While remaining an ordained Christian minister, she has found herself "nourished" by the names and images with which the native Mayan religions address God:

"Heart of the Sky"
"Mother and Father of Life"
"Heart of the Earth"
"Our Common Material Origin"
"Most Profound of I Am I Am"
"Includer of Everything."[24]

INCLUDER OF EVERYTHING, EVER PRESENT, EVER ACCOMPANYING

At the name "Includer of Everything" the cloud breaks into spontaneous Amens, while we who worship in the church under reconstruction pray,

Lord, my heart is not large enough,
my memory is not good enough,
my will is not strong enough:
Take my heart and enlarge it,

Take my memory and give it quicker recall,
Take my will and make it strong
    and make me conscious of thee
        everpresent,
            ever accompanying.[25]

While we pray, we hear the rush of the Wind yet again, and gazing through the God-shaped hole we realize that we are not simply looking upward, we are also looking downward. For all directions are simultaneously the opposite within the "Includer of Everything," the one in whom "we live and move and have our being" (Acts 17:28). From other points in the universe our "up" is "down," our "in" is "out." As Rainer Maria Rilke reflects,

Perhaps we are *above*,
woven into the skies of other beings
who gaze toward us at evening. Perhaps their
poets praise us. Perhaps some of them
pray up toward us. Perhaps we are the aim
of strange curses that never reach us,
neighbors of a god whom they envision
in our heights when they weep alone,
whom they believe in and whom they lose,
and whose image, like a gleam from their
seeking lamps, fleeting and then gone,
passes over our scattered faces.[26]

Perhaps. But even if not, the act of imagining it to be so expands the landscape of the heart and reminds us of our connection and responsibility to all that is. For we are in fact made out of star dust and we are connected to all that was and is and is to be.

At this very thought the cloud gathers in greater strength than ever before, and while I listen to the witnesses singing their songs from across the ages, my conviction grows that it is better to leave the God-shaped hole open than to fill it in. The role of visionary preachers in a fragmented world is not to insist on this or that image of God as the ultimate

revelation. The role of visionary preachers is to keep
the church perpetually open to the polyphonic
Spirit, to keep enlightening and expanding the landscape of the heart.

I hear the voice of Nathan the prophet reminding
me that it was never God's idea in the first place to
live in an enclosed temple: "Thus says the Lord: Are
you the one to build me a house to live in? . . . did
I ever speak a word . . . saying, 'Why have you not
built me a house of cedar?' " (2 Samuel 7:5-7).

> At the speaking of the prophet, the songs of the
>   cloud
> move beyond the vast cavern of the church under
>   reconstruction
> and the vibrations of the sound become one
> with the light waves of the stars
> while we look down by looking up
> while we look out by looking in
> while we sing by keeping silence
> while we hear the soundless music
> of the everlasting choir that without interruption
>   offers
> a polyphonic unison harmonized cacophonous
>   chorus
> to the one who in the bleak midwinter
> when frosty wind made moan
> battered our hearts as a three personed God
> who identifies with us
> and asks us on the wind
> if we were there when they crucified my Lord
> and if we have searched to find the true cross
> and discovered
> that we are sometimes asleep through the resur-
>   rection
> and sometimes awake
> in a posture of prayer

not anxious about staying in control
but only wanting to receive and follow the risen
  Christ
who is the poem itself that becomes in us
the poem of our life
through every word and deed of compassion and
  justice
till all we are spells the word of God
so that through our daily life
as well as our sermons as visionary preachers
the wind blows and carries the voices and visions
that heal the fragmented world
and that make the church under reconstruction
a launching point for exploration
beyond the shadowed and contracted landscape
  of the heart
toward a universe of wonder
where we live knowing
we are connected to a love that nothing
not even death
can separate us from
and we fill with such gratitude
that there flows through all the dancing atoms of
  our bodies
the eternal rapturous lyric springing from the
  deep dear core of things in one constant but
  continually modulated lament and hymn of
  praise Hallelujah, Hallelujah, Hallelujah. . . .

Notes

1. THE CHURCH UNDER RECONSTRUCTION

1. Poem, copyright 1997, Thomas H. Troeger. Although the poem is my original work, I took the image of the "God-shaped hole" from Wendy Steiner, *The Scandal of Pleasure: Art in an Age of Fundamentalism* (Chicago: University of Chicago Press, 1995), p. 114.

2. Arthur Van Seters, "Daring to Address Our Times: Preaching as a Social Act, the Continuing Agenda," an unpublished paper for the Academy of Homiletics, December 1997, p. 4. The paper is a reflective sequel to the book that Van Seters edited a decade earlier on related themes: *Preaching as a Social Act* (Nashville: Abingdon Press, 1988).

3. Loren B. Mead, *Reinventing the Congregation for a New Mission Frontier*, The Once and Future Church Series (Bethesda, Md.: The Alban Institute, 1991), pp. 28-29. I also am indebted in this section to workshop/conferences I have attended on church leadership sponsored by the Center for Parish Development.

4. Ibid., p. 43. Emphasis is Mead's. I am also drawing here upon Donald E. Miller, *Reinventing American Protestantism: Christianity in the New Millennium* (Berkeley: University of California Press, 1997).

5. I am quoting from James McAuley, "Journey into Egypt," in *James McAuley: Poetry, Essays, and Personal Commentary*, ed. Leonie Kramer (St. Lucia: University of Queensland Press, 1988), p. 190. The original quotation appears in Wladimir Weidle, *Les Abeilles d'Aristee* (Paris, 1954), p. 289.

6. Mary Ann Wiesemann-Mills, O.P., at the Academy of Homiletics, Santa Fe, New Mexico, 2 December 1996. She drew the concept of "impasse" from Constance FitzGerald, O.C.D., "Impasse and Dark Night," in *Women's Spirituality: Resources for Christian Development*, ed. Joann Walski Conn (New York: Paulist Press, 1986). The image of God holding us in her womb came in part from Elizabeth Johnson, *She Who Is: The Mystery of God in Theological Feminist Discourse* (New York: Crossroad Publishing, 1992), pp. 233-36.

7. Mead, *Reinventing the Congregation*, p. 54.

8. Jung Young Lee, *Korean Preaching: An Interpretation* (Nashville: Abingdon Press, 1997), p. 48.

9. Harry Baker Adams, *Preaching: The Burden and the Joy* (St. Louis: Chalice Press, 1996), p. 43.

10. Don E. Saliers, *Worship as Theology: Foretaste of Glory Divine* (Nashville: Abingdon Press, 1994), p. 86.

11. Harry Eskew and Hugh T. McElrath, *Sing with Understanding: An Introduction to Christian Hymnology* (Nashville: Broadman Press, 1980), p. 59.

12. Erik Routley, chapter 8 in *With Tongues of Fire: Profiles in Twentieth-Century Hymn Writing*, ed. Paul Westermeyer (St. Louis: Concordia Publishing House, 1995), 119-20. This is a republication of the first chapter of Routley's original work *Christian Hymns Observed: When in Our Music God Is Glorified* (Princeton: Prestige Publications, Inc., 1982).

13. Erik Routley, *A Panorama of Christian Hymnody* (Chicago: G. I. A. Publications, Inc., 1979), p. 55. For a lively summary of this tradition which includes texts in Latin with English translation, see pp. 55-77.

14. Miller, *Reinventing American Protestantism*, p. 187.

15. Ada Maria Isasi-Diaz, *Mujerista Theology: A Theology for the Twenty-First Century* (Maryknoll, N.Y.: Orbis Books, 1996), p. 3.

16. John Donne, "An Anatomy of the World: The First Anniversary" in *The Complete Poetry and Selected Prose of John Donne*, ed. Charles M. Coffin (New York: The Modern Library, 1952), p. 191.

17. The International Commission on English in the Liturgy, *The Psalter: A Faithful and Inclusive Rendering from the Hebrew into Contemporary English Poetry* (Chicago: Liturgy Training Publications, 1995), paginated by psalm number.

18. Mieke Bal, *On Story-Telling: Essays in Narratology*, ed. David Jobling (Sonoma, Calif.: Polebridge, 1991), p. 14.

19. *The HarperCollins Study Bible, New Revised Standard Version*, ed. Wayne A. Meeks (New York: HarperCollins Publishers, 1993), p. 2170. See Romans 8:29, 1 Corinthians 15:49, 2 Corinthians 3:18, Colossians 3:10.

20. Alfred Kazin, *God and the American Writer* (New York: Alfred A. Knopf, 1997), p. 187.

21. Jerome J. Langford, *Galileo, Science, and the Church*, 3rd ed. (Ann Arbor: University of Michigan Press, 1992), p. 161. Emphasis added.

22. Ibid., p. 84.

23. For a moving, positive interpretation of this psalm that is rooted in a contemporary experience of exile, see Isasi-Diaz, "'By the Rivers of Babylon': Exile as a Way of Life," in *Mujerista Theology*, pp. 35-56. I do not believe it is necessary to choose between the two interpretations, deciding that one is right and the other wrong. Following Isasi-Diaz, I would say the difference lies in "one's perspective and purpose when dealing with any biblical text" (p. 37).

24. Gail R. O'Day, "John," in *The Women's Bible Commentary*, ed. Carol A. Newsom and Sharon H. Ringe (Louisville: Westminster/John Knox Press, 1992), p. 301.

25. Peter J. Gomes, *The Good Book: Reading the Bible with Mind and Heart* (New York: William Morrow and Company, 1996), p. 40.

26. Ronald J. Allen, "Why Preach from Passages in the Bible?" in *Preaching as a Theological Task: World, Gospel, Scripture*, ed. Thomas G. Long and Edward Farley (Louisville: Westminster/John Knox Press, 1996), p. 179.

27. Jo Ringgenberg, "A Question," in *Re-Membering and Re-Imagining*, ed. Nancy J. Berneking and Pamela Carter Joern (Cleveland: The Pilgrim Press, 1995), p. 225.

28. Rudolf Bohren, "Practical Theology as a Critique of Knowledge," in *Preaching as a Theological Task*, p. 59.

29. Ibid., p. 65.

30. Erik Routley, *The Divine Formula: A Book for Worshipers, Preachers, and Musicians and All Who Celebrate the Mysteries* (Princeton: Prestige Publications, 1985), p. 91.

31. Gjertrud Schnackenberg, "The Epistle of Paul the Apostle to the Colossians," in *Incarnation: Contemporary Writers on the New Testament*, ed. Alfred Corn (New York: Viking Books, 1990), pp. 209-10. Emphasis added.

32. I am quoting Abraham Joshua Heschel, as found in Alice Parker, *Melodious Accord: Good Singing in Church* (Chicago: Liturgy Training Publications, 1991), p. 11. The original place of publication or speaking is not given.

33. *The Oxford Book of Prayer*, ed. George Appleton (New York: Oxford University Press, 1985), p. 293. The full prayer begins with greater anguish than is true of my own soul: "Ah, Lord, the torment of this task that Thou hast laid on me."

34. Bohren, "Practical Theology," p. 67. He is quoting here from Peter Stuhlmacher, "Spiritual Exegesis?" in *Einfach von Gott reden: Ein Theologischer Diskus* (Stuttgart: W. Kohlhammer, 1994), precise page number not given.

35. Ibid., p. 65.

36. Ibid.

37. Steiner, *The Scandal of Pleasure*, p. 109.

38. Bernard Shaw, *Saint Joan: A Chronicle Play in Six Scenes and an Epilogue* (Baltimore: Penguin Books, 1964), p. 59.

39. I amalgamate the three words as a way of suggesting the fusion of these realities which is conveyed in the Hebrew and Greek but lost in English translation.

40. David Rosenberg, *A Poet's Bible: Rediscovering Voices of the Original Text* (New York: Hyperion, 1991), p. xviii.

41. The phrase "imaginative accuracy" was suggested by Rosenberg's judgment that "the official translations of the Bible today are imaginatively inaccurate," p. xviii.

42. Christina Rossetti, *Poems and Prose*, ed. Jan Marsh (Rutland, Vt.: Everyman, 1994), p. 109. The carol appears in nearly every major English language hymnal.

43. *The Oxford Companion to English Literature*, ed. Margaret Drabble, 5th ed. (New York: Oxford University Press, 1985), p. 255.

44. Eugene Lowry, *The Sermon: Dancing the Edge of Mystery* (Nashville: Abingdon Press, 1997). Lowry has written so many books on the nature of how sermons engage and carry us along through a process of discovery and insight that it is difficult to settle upon one. But this most recent work summarizes his thought in addition to providing a fine survey of literature on the subject.

45. Jan Marsh, *Christina Rossetti: A Writer's Life* (New York: Viking, 1994), p. 284.

46. Ibid., pp. 415-16.

47. Paul Scott Wilson, *Imagination of the Heart: New Understandings in Preaching* (Nashville: Abingdon Press, 1988), pp. 33-34.

48. Wendell Berry, *Standing by Words: Essays* (San Francisco: North Point Press, 1983), pp. 204-5.

49. The Rev. Dr. Harold T. Lewis, a member of the rectors of churches belonging to The Consortium of Endowed Episcopal Parishes, February 19, 1998.

50. I am indebted to one of my manuscript readers, Professor Delwin Brown, for pointing out the need to name this sixth principle.

51. Frank Burch Brown, *Transfiguration: Poetic Metaphor and the Languages of Religious Belief* (Chapel Hill: The University of North Carolina Press, 1983), p. 176.

52. Lowry, *The Sermon*, p. 43.

53. Alfred Delp as quoted by Bohren in "Practical Theology," p. 64.

54. Thomas H. Troeger, *Borrowed Light: Hymn Texts, Prayers, and Poems* (New York: Oxford University Press, 1994), p. 123.

55. For an analysis of how sound fuses with thought in African American preaching, see Evans Crawford, *The Hum: Call and Response in African American Preaching* (Nashville: Abingdon Press, 1995). Although I wrote "the hummings in the soul" several years before reading Crawford's work, his description of "hum thought" (pp. 49-60) is close in spirit to the reality I suggest in my poem.

56. Rollo May, *The Courage to Create* (New York: Norton, 1994), p. 11.

2. THE SPIRIT SIGHS:
SEARCH FOR THE TRUE CROSS

1. *The Oxford Dictionary of World Religions*, ed. John Bowker (New York: Oxford University Press, 1997), s.v. "Cross."

2. Jan Willem Drijvers, *Helena Augusta: The Mother of Constantine the Great and the Legend of Her Finding of the True Cross* (Leiden, The Netherlands: E. J. Brill, 1992), p. 5. I am indebted to this book for much of the discussion of the legend. For a precis see "Finding of the True Cross" in Diane Apostolos-Cappadona, *Dictionary of Christian Art* (New York: Continuum, 1994), p. 132.

3. Drijvers, *Helena Augusta*, p. 16.

4. The dates of birth and death for Gelasius are not known.

5. All the direct quotations of the legend are from Drijvers, *Helena Augusta*, pp. 79-80. He believes this text "comes closest to the original," although it is important to remember that the legend was very flexible and probably had multiple oral forms as well as its many written variations.

6. Apostolos-Cappadona, *Dictionary of Christian Art*, p. 93.

7. Ibid., p. 132.

8. Drijvers, *Helena Augusta*, p. 81.

9. Ibid.

10. Joseph M. Webb, "Pluralism and the Search for a 'New Gospel' " in the *Papers of the Annual Meeting: The Academy of Homiletics*, December 4-6, 1997, p. 56. Webb's paper is based on material for a book to be published by Chalice Press and tentatively titled *Pluralism in the Pulpit: Reworking the Gospel for Postmodern Preaching.*

11. For a helpful discussion of the theological and pastoral differences between being healed and being cured see Kathy Black, *A Healing Homiletic: Preaching and Disability* (Nashville: Abingdon Press, 1996). Black demonstrates how to honor the human wholeness of people with disabling conditions. Her wisdom about how to preach on the healing stories in the gospel applies equally to a story like the legend of finding the true cross.

12. The poster can be found in *Dietrich Bonhoeffer: A Life in Pictures*, ed. Eberhard Bethge, Renate Bethge, and Christian Gremmels, trans. John Bowden (Philadelphia: Fortress Press, 1986), p. 122.

13. I am indebted to Paul Millette, the research librarian at the Iliff School of Theology, for gathering this material on Helmut Herzfeld.

14. Drijvers, *Helena Augusta*, p. 144.

15. Ibid., pp. 187-88.

16. Ada Maria Isasi-Diaz, *Mujerista Theology: A Theology for the Twenty-First Century* (Maryknoll, N.Y.: Orbis Books, 1996), p. 63.

17. Christine M. Smith, *Preaching as Weeping, Confession, and Resistance: Radical Responses to Radical Evil* (Louisville: Westminster/John Knox Press, 1992), p. 153.

18. Harry Baker Adams, *Preaching: The Burden and the Joy* (St. Louis: Chalice Press, 1996), p. 46.

19. James Henley Thornwell as quoted in Alfred Kazin, *God and the American Writer* (New York: Alfred A. Knopf, 1997), p. 129.

20. Henry Bettenson, *Documents of the Christian Church* (New York: Oxford University Press, 1947), p. 40. Emphasis added.

21. Tree imagery for the cross is common in the New Testament: Acts 5:30; 10:39; 13:29; Galatians 3:13; 1 Peter 2:24. All speak of Christ being killed on the tree. Paul uses the

image in Galatians 3:13 as a way of interpreting what Christ has done to the law by citing Deuteronomy 21:23: "Cursed is everyone who hangs on a tree." The second stanza of the spiritual asks: "Were you there when they nailed him to the tree?"

22. David Buttrick, *A Captive Voice: The Liberation of Preaching* (Louisville: Westminster/John Knox Press, 1994), p. 13.

23. Philip and Sally Scharper, *The Gospel in Art by the Peasants of Solentiname* (Maryknoll, N.Y.: Orbis Books, 1984), p. 60.

24. Johann Baptist Metz, *Faith in History and Society* (New York: Seabury Press, 1980), p. 66.

25. Walter J. Burghardt, S.J., "Advent: Remember, Repent, Rehearse" in *The Living Pulpit* 6, no. 4 (October-December 1997), p. 5.

26. Sallie McFague, *Metaphorical Theology: Models of God in Religious Language* (Philadelphia: Fortress Press, 1982), p. 29.

27. *A Testament to Freedom: The Essential Writings of Dietrich Bonhoeffer*, ed. Geffrey B. Kelly and F. Burton Nelson, rev. ed. (San Francisco: HarperSF, 1995), p. 14. All page numbers to the quotations from and about Bonhoeffer refer to this volume unless otherwise noted.

28. Dietrich Bonhoeffer, *The Cost of Discipleship*, trans. R. H. Fuller (New York: Macmillan, 1963), pp. 45-47.

29. Dietrich Bonhoeffer, *Letters and Papers from Prison*, enlarged ed., trans. R. H. Fuller et al. (New York: Macmillan, 1971), p. 17.

30. Ibid., p. 13.

31. Ibid., pp. 15-16.

32. *Love Letters from Cell 92: The Correspondence Between Dietrich Bonhoeffer and Maria von Wedemeyer 1943–45*, ed. Ruth-Alice von Bismarck and Ulrich Kabitz, trans. John Brownjohn (Nashville: Abingdon Press, 1995), p. 64.

33. Dietrich Bonhoeffer, "Who Am I?" in *Letters and Papers*, pp. 347-48. I provide another analysis of this poem in *Creating Fresh Images for Preaching: New Rungs for Jacob's Ladder* (Valley Forge: Judson Press, 1982), pp. 69-70. The poem haunts me and I believe will haunt me for my whole life.

34. *Dietrich Bonhoeffer: A Life in Pictures*, p. 233.

35. Ibid.

36. Ronald J. Allen, "Truth in the Postmodern World" in Ronald J. Allen, Barbara Shires Blaisdell, and Scott Black Johnston, *Theology for Preaching: Authority, Truth, and Knowledge of God in a Postmodern Ethos* (Nashville: Abingdon Press, 1997), p. 67.

37. Dietrich Bonhoeffer, *Letters and Papers,* pp. 400-401.

3. THE SPIRIT SIGHS: FOLLOW THE LIVING CHRIST

1. The image is available in Yves Christe et al., *Art of the Christian World A.D. 200–1500: A Handbook of Styles and Forms* (New York: Rizzoli, 1982), p. 44. I am deeply indebted to the Rev. Richard Manzelmann who first introduced me to this visual motif through an Easter sermon about twenty-five years ago. The image has haunted me ever since that sermon.

2. Scott Black Johnston in Ronald J. Allen, Barbara Shires Blaisdell, and Scott Black Johnston, *Theology for Preaching: Authority, Truth, and Knowledge of God in a Postmodern Ethos* (Nashville: Abingdon Press, 1997), p. 75.

3. Donald K. McKim, "The Gospel as Empowered Speech for Proclamation and Persuasion" in *Preaching as a Theological Task: World, Gospel, Scripture,* ed. Thomas G. Long and Edward Farley (Louisville: Westminster/John Knox Press, 1996), p. 125.

4. H. A. Williams, *True Resurrection* (New York: Holt, Rinehart, and Winston, 1972), p. 10.

5. Edward Farley, "Toward a New Paradigm for Preaching," in *Preaching as a Theological Task,* p. 165.

6. Ronald J. Allen, "Why Preach from Passages in the Bible?" in *Preaching as a Theological Task,* p. 177.

7. P. T. Forsyth, as quoted by McKim in "The Gospel as Empowered Speech," p. 124.

8. Brian Wren, "Christ Is Alive," in *The United Methodist Hymnal* (Nashville: The United Methodist Publishing House, 1989), no. 318. Also in many other recent hymnals. The text given here is Wren's latest revision.

9. Valerie Brown Troutman in a panel discussion about ministry during the Academy of Homiletics annual meeting, Oakland, California, December 1997.

10. David Buttrick, *Homiletic: Moves and Structures* (Philadelphia: Fortress Press, 1987), p. 18.

11. Peter J. Gomes, *The Good Book: Reading the Bible with*

Mind and Heart (New York: William Morrow and Company, 1996), p. 82.

12. David Daiches, *God and the Poets* (Oxford: Clarendon Press, 1984), p. 34.

13. Letty M. Russell, "Introduction: Liberating the Word" in *Feminist Interpretation of the Bible* (Philadelphia: The Westminster Press, 1985), p. 17. Emphasis is Russell's.

14. Frederick Buechner, *The Magnificent Defeat* (New York: Seabury Press, 1966), pp. 76-77.

15. Ingmar Bergman, *Images: My Life in Film*, trans. Marianne Ruuth (New York: Arcade Publishing, 1994), p. 67.

16. Ibid., pp. 236 and 258.

17. Zbigniew Herbert, "Meditations of Mr. Cogito on Redemption" from *Mr. Cogito*, trans. John Carpenter and Bogdana Carpenter (Hopewell, N.J.: Ecco Press, 1993), p. 50.

18. David F. Noble, *The Religion of Technology: The Divinity of Man and the Spirit of Invention* (New York: Alfred A. Knopf, 1997). All the page numbers following quotations in this section are from Noble.

19. Colleen Cordes, "As Educators Rush to Embrace Technology, a Coterie of Skeptics Seeks to Be Heard" in *Chronicle of Higher Education* 44, no. 19 (16 January 1998), p. A26.

20. Melva Wilson Costen, *African American Christian Worship* (Nashville: Abingdon Press, 1993), p. 21.

21. Cordes, "As Educators Rush," p. A26.

22. George Appleton, from *One Man's Prayers* (London: S.P.C.K., 1967).

23. See chapter 1 underneath "Finding Meaning in a Fragmented Age."

24. Delwin Brown, commenting on an earlier draft of this chapter.

25. John Donne, "Death's Duell, or A Consolation to the Soule, Against the Dying Life, and Living Death of the Body" in *The Complete Poetry and Selected Prose of John Donne*, ed. Charles M. Coffin (New York: The Modern Library, 1952), p. 587. Italics and spellings are as they are printed in Coffin's collection. All quotations from Donne's works are taken from this volume unless otherwise noted.

26. I am indebted to the following works for my account of Donne's life and work: John Carey, *John Donne: Life, Mind, and Art* (London: Faber and Faber, 1990). Helen Gardner, *John Donne: a Collection of Critical Essays* (Englewood Cliffs, N.J.: Prentice-Hall. 1962). Derek Parker, *John Donne and His*

World (London: Thames and Hudson, 1975). The Parker book, which includes many period illustrations of Donne and his time in European history, was especially helpful in gaining a vivid sense of Donne as a living person.
27. Carey, *John Donne: Life, Mind, and Art*, p. xiv.
28. C. H. Sisson, "A Letter to John Donne" in *Selected Poems* (New York: New Directions, 1995).
29. Parker, *John Donne and His World*, p. 69.
30. There are two settings of this hymn in the Episcopal hymnal. Although challenging for many congregations, they could easily be offered as an anthem or solo if you do not have a strong singing congregation.
31. Sisson, "A Letter."

4. THE SPIRIT SIGHS: EXPAND AND ENLIGHTEN THE LANDSCAPE OF THE HEART

1. The International Commission on English in the Liturgy, *The Psalter: A Faithful and Inclusive Rendering from the Hebrew into Contemporary English Poetry* (Chicago: Liturgy Training Publications, 1994). Pages are marked by Psalm numbers.
2. *Harper's Bible Dictionary*, ed. Paul J. Achtemeier (San Francisco: HarperSF, 1985), s.v. "firmament."
3. J. B. S. Haldane, cited without reference in *The National Geographic Atlas of the World*, 5th ed. (Washington, D.C.: National Geographic Society, 1981), p. 6.
4. Ibid., p. 7.
5. James McAuley, "An Art of Poetry" in *Collected Poems* (Sydney: Angus & Robertson, 1994).
6. Leonora Tubbs Tisdale, *Preaching as Local Theology and Folk Art* (Minneapolis: Fortress Press, 1997), p. 43. The italics are Tisdale's to indicate she is drawing upon David Kelsey, *The Uses of Scripture in Recent Theology* (Philadelphia: Fortress Press, 1975).
7. Garrett Green, *Imagining God: Theology and the Religious Imagination* (San Francisco: Harper & Row, 1989), p. 6.
8. Jennie Hargraves Nampijinpa, in *Inside Black Australia: An Anthology of Aboriginal Poetry*, ed. Kevin Gilbert (Ringwood, Australia: Penguin Books, 1988), p. 22.
9. I am indebted throughout this section to Tisdale's work, although I am developing the themes in my own way.
10. *Harper's Bible Dictionary*, s.v. "logos."

11. Samuel Laeuchli, "The Expulsion from the Garden and the Hermeneutics of Play," in *Body and Bible: Interpreting and Experiencing Biblical Narratives*, ed. Bjorn Krondorfer (Philadelphia: Trinity Press International, 1992), p. 35.

12. Robert J. Schreiter, *Constructing Local Theologies* (Maryknoll, N.Y.: Orbis Books, 1985), 29.

13. Ibid., p. 14.

14. Ibid., p. 19.

15. Ibid., p. 21.

16. Jean de Brebeuf, "Twas in the Moon of Wintertime," trans. Jesse Edgar Middleton, in *The United Methodist Hymnal* (Nashville: The United Methodist Publishing House, 1989), no. 244. This hymn may also be found in many other recent hymnals including *The Presbyterian Hymnal* and *The New Century Hymnal*.

17. Lionel Adey, *Hymns and the Christian "Myth"* (Vancouver: University of British Columbia Press, 1986), pp. 99-100.

18. Sallie McFague, *Metaphorical Theology: Models of God in Religious Language* (Philadelphia: Fortress Press, 1982), p. 120.

19. David J. Bryant, *Faith and the Play of the Imagination: On the Role of Imagination in Religion* (Macon, Ga.: Mercer University Press, 1989), p. 53.

20. Richard Davenport-Hines, *Auden* (New York: Pantheon Books, 1996), p. 151.

21. A number of recent works in homiletics lead preachers through the process of developing their imaginative powers in ways that balance freedom and rules, including the following: Eduard R. Riegert, *Imaginative Shock: Preaching and Metaphor* (Burlington, Ontario: Trinity Press, 1990). Thomas H. Troeger, *Imagining a Sermon* (Nashville: Abingdon Press, 1990). James A. Wallace, *Imaginal Preaching: An Archetypal Perspective* (Mahwah, N.J.: Paulist Press, 1995). Paul Scott Wilson, *Imagination of the Heart: New Understanding in Preaching* (Nashville: Abingdon Press, 1988). In addition to these works, the following do not focus so exclusively on the imagination in preaching but still offer approaches to the interpretation of scripture and experience that have profound consequences for the homiletical imagination in our fragmented age: Evans Crawford, *The Hum* (Nashville: Abingdon Press, 1995). *Body and Bible: Interpreting and Experiencing Biblical Narratives*, ed. Bjorn Krondorfer (Philadelphia: Trinity Press International, 1992). Sallie McFague, *Metaphorical Theology: Models of God in Religious*

Language (Philadelphia: Fortress Press, 1982). Philip and Sally Scharper, eds., *The Gospel in Art by the Peasants of Solentiname* (Maryknoll, N.Y.: Orbis Books, 1984). Miriam Therese Winter, *Woman Prayer, Woman Song: Resources for Ritual* (Philadelphia: Medical Missionary Sisters, 1987).

22. John Hollander, *The Work of Poetry* (New York: Columbia University Press, 1997), p. 145.

23. No. 682 in *The United Methodist Hymnal.* It continues to be reprinted in nearly every denomination's hymnal.

24. These quotations are from my notes of an interview and conversation of September 4, 1996, between Julia Esquivel and the faculty members of the Iliff School of Theology who traveled to Guatemala under a grant from the United Methodist Board of Global Ministries.

25. *The Oxford Book of Prayer*, ed. George Appleton (New York: Oxford University Press, 1985), p. 55. The editor is author of the prayer.

26. Rainer Maria Rilke, "About Fountains," in *The Book of Images: A Bilingual Edition*, trans. Edward Snow (San Francisco: North Point Press, 1991), pp. 205 and 207. The quoted lines are continuous; the intermediate page, 206, is the original German text.